P9-EEE-362

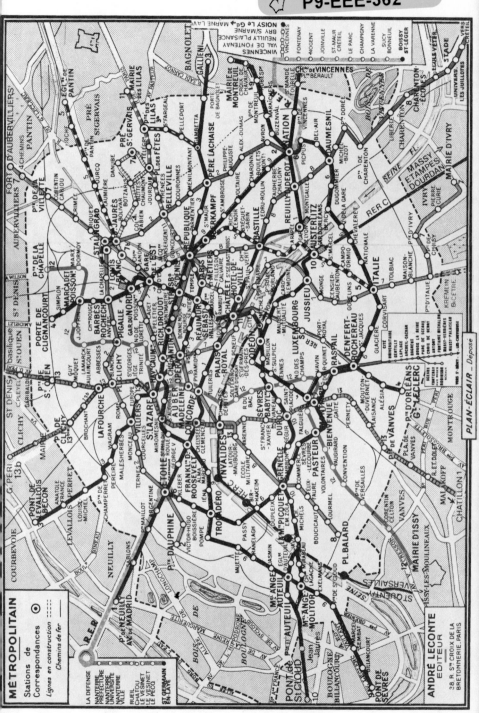

Paris *Confidential*

by Warren and Jean Trabant

Edited by Elizabeth W. Philip

Agora Inc.
824 E. Baltimore Street
Baltimore, MD 21202

Paris
Confidential

Publisher: William Bonner
Managing Editor: Kathleen Murphy
Style Editor: Kathleen Peddicord
Graphic Designer: Becky Mangus
Cover Design: Jack French
Typesetters: Elizabeth Cox and Denise Plowman
Research Assistant: Terry Ciofalo

Cover painting, *Paris, A Rainy Day*, by Gustave Caillebotte; it
shows the intersection of la rue de Turin and la rue de Moscou.
Courtesy of The Art Institute of Chicago.

ISBN: 0-945332-00-9

Table of Contents

Chapter I: Welcome to Paris. **1**
Paris Lights. 1
Some Background. 2
Le Cafe: a French Institution. 5
French Social Customs. 6
Who are the French?. 6

Chapter II: Paris by *Arrondissement* **7**
The 1st, 2nd, 3rd, and 4th *Arrondissements* 7
The 5th, 6th, and 7th *Arrondissements*. 18
The 8th and 9th *Arrondissements*. 31
The 10th, 11th, and 12th *Arrondissements* 36
The 13th, 14th, and 15th *Arrondissements*. 39
The 16th and 17th *Arrondissements*. 47
The 18th, 19th, and 20th *Arrondissements*. 53
La Défense. 60
Chinatown. 61
A Guide to Buying Real Estate in Paris. 63

Chapter III: Finding French Cuisine. **67**
The Covered Markets of Paris. 67
At an Open Street Market. 68
What's Cooking?. 70
Non-French Food. 71
A History of the Restaurant. 72
At Table With the French. 72
The Great Restaurants of Paris. 74

Chapter IV: Shopping in Paris. **77**
La Papeterie. 77
Art Supplies. 77
Toys. 78
Jewelry. 78
Antique Clothes. 78
Clothing for Men and Women. 78
Children's Clothing. 79

Off-price Clothing for Men, Women, and Children. 80
Bathroom and Dressing Table Accessories. 80
Needlepoint/*Merceries*. 80
Books. 80
Special Gifts. 81
Museum Shops. 81
The Department Stores. 82
For Collectors. 83
Les Passages of Paris. 84
Le Marché aux Puces—Paris' Flea Market. 86

Chapter V: When You Visit Paris. 89
Hotels. 89
The Star System: Details. 92
How to Use Paris Post Offices. 93
The Public Toilet: a History and Guide. 94
The Best Restaurant Toliets (and Telephone Facilities). 95
Reading a Map of Paris. 96
The Best Way to Tote Your Stuff. 98

Chapter VI: Filling Your Paris Days. 101
Learning the Language. 102
Being Buried. 103
The Museums of Paris. 103
Jobs in France. 105
In the Swim. 105
The American Library in Paris. 106

Chapter VII: Getting Around Paris. 107
The RER. 108
Life in the Underground. 108
The City Bus System. 109
Paris by Bike. 110
Cabbing It. 111
SITU—the Automatic Transit Consultant. 111
Sightseeing in Paris on City Buses. 111
Nine Scenic Bus Routes. 112
Mr. Bus Stop. 133
Getting Out of Paris on the SNCF. 134
Hiking in France. 134

Foreword

Paris has such a remarkable reputation that it practically invites disappointment. To first-time visitors, it may not seem all it's cracked up to be. As Somerset Maughan wrote (about different cities), "When you leave them it is with a feeling that you have missed something, and you cannot help thinking that they have some secret that they have kept from you."

It has been a long time since I lived in Paris. Things change. At first glance, the city is neither as beautiful nor intriguing as I remember. Perhaps the city has regressed to the mean, I tell myself, no longer extraordinary...like a child prodigy who grows to middle age and becomes a fairly run-of-the-mill citizen.

Has Paris changed? Is it really less exciting and less interesting than it was in my youth? Or do I no longer hold the key to the inner city and the secrets waiting to be discovered there?

Fortunately, Warren and Jean Trabant have answered that question. Their new book shows that Paris is still Paris.

They know the city as insiders...and can introduce you to it in a way that you could never get from a standard tourist guidebook.

This is not just another guide to Paris. And it is not a guide for just casual tourists. This is a guide for those who really want to get to know the heart and soul of this exciting city. In short, it shows you how to get to know Paris as true connoisseurs know it.

Paris is a city with many secrets and many charms. And some of its most enchanting aspects are those that are least explored and least appreciated by most tourists. There is a city within the city...a rich and exciting, *private* city...a hidden world available only to insiders who know where to go and what to do...a secret, fascinating city that most visitors never see.

Paris Confidential takes you through the city, *arrondissement* by *arrondissement*. It gives insights and information that even most life-long Parisians don't know.

What makes this book exceptional is that it focuses on what is *exceptional*...unique...different. After all, that is what makes the world worth exploring...the *differences*. You can eat in McDonalds or Burger King...or stay at the Hyatt...in almost any city in the world. But only in Paris can you eat at Chez Pauline on la rue Villedo. It has been in business for more than 30 years...handed down from father to son. And it is one of the few restaurants in France where one can eat a soup called Billy By, made with cream and mussels.

It is these one-of-a-kind features that make Paris...or any city... special. And these are the points that Warren and Jean Trabant have discovered, explored, and described with unerring accuracy and shrewd insight.

William Chamberlayne

Introduction

More than a score of guides on Paris are published each year in French or English. For the most part, they cover the tourist sites, the museums, the hotels, and the restaurants that border the river Seine. Many visitors never venture north of l'Opéra or south of le boulevard Montparnasse. Most of Paris remains a mystery.

This book is not designed to attract anyone away from what has made Paris one of the most fascinating cities of the world. Rather it is intended to supplement visits with information about the lesser-known neighborhoods and things to do and see in all Paris.

We suggest that in addition to our guide, you arm yourself with the *Michelin Green Guide to Paris*. In our opinion, it is the best for seeing the tourist sites. It has good descriptions of all the monuments, historical data, maps, and tourist itineraries. There is no other guide that does that sort of thing quite as well. The *Michelin Paris et Sa Banlieue*, an extract from the *Guide to the Hotels and Restaurants of France* (red cover), provides the most serious list of restaurants and hotels in Paris. (Our criticism of this guide is that most of the prices for restaurant meals are on the low side. Add 10% to each for more accuracy.)

Then there is a little book of maps called *Plan de Paris par Arrondissements et Communes de Banlieue Avec la Station du Métro la Plus Proche*, which simply means that it is a complete set of maps, one of each *arrondissement* of Paris (there are 20) and one for each close suburb. It also provides a list of streets with map coordinates and where to find the beginning and end of each one. The book also includes a map of the metro, details on the routes of all Paris city buses, a list of embassies, consulates, legations, post offices, police stations, churches, schools, city halls (each *arrondissement* has one), ministries, museums, monuments, and useful addresses. One edition of this handy little volume is called "indispensable." As you will learn, that is exactly what it is. Several editions are available. We recommend the one published by LeConte. It is available in almost all bookstores and newspaper kiosks throughout Paris.

With these three guides plus the one you are now reading, you will be able to do Paris as you wish and in great detail. All are easy to carry with you.

Bon voyage!

Chapter I

Welcome to Paris

Everyone—he who knows Paris well and he who has never been here—has his own idea of Paris. Each is different.

Hemingway fans probably see Paris as a city of sidewalk cafes, little restaurants, and an English-language lending library frequented by creative writers, most of them American. Elliot Paul describes narrow winding streets and quaint shopkeepers. Harold Loeb tells about a town of little magazines, publishers, writers, and poets. F. Scott Fitzgerald's Paris was one of glamorous people crowding bars and chic restaurants. Paris is all these places. It is, in some ways, the quintessential city, made rich through commerce, entrepreneurship, and the wealth of aristocrats. It has been for centuries a center for scholarship and thought and a haven for artists and their finest works.

Paris Lights

Sometimes referred to as the City of Light, Paris had only three street lights in 1318: one on l'Arc du Grand-Châtelet; one on la Tour

The Seine, between la Cité and the quay of the Augustins.

de Nesle; and one at le Cimetière des Innocents. Parisians who went out at night carried torches or lanterns or had servants who carried them.

In three different periods during the first half of the 16th century, ordinances required that each house, between 9 p.m. and midnight, have a candle in one of its ground-floor windows—"to avoid the dangers of *les mauvais garçons* who roam at night in the city." The candles had little effect, as each night during that time the watchmen would find 15 or so bodies in the street.

L'Abbé Caraffe, in 1662, introduced a mobile lamp. On certain street corners, lamp porters lined up, like taxis do today, offering to light the way for 5 sous for each slice of candle consumed (candles were divided into six parts). Lamp porters with oil lamps carried hourglasses for timing—3 sous for every 15 minutes of lighting. They took their clients to the doors of their apartments, even if they had to climb seven flights of stairs.

One of Madame de Sévigné's 1672 letters read, "We found it pleasant taking Madame Scarron home at midnight, to le faubourg Saint-Germain. We returned gaily, thanks to the lanterns that were a security against thieves."

Toward 1700, lanterns were suspended on walls with a rope and pulley. This means of lighting had its inconveniences. The light was often extinguished by the wind, and the smoke dirtied the windows. These lanterns were not used on moonlit nights or during the summer. In 1729, the city of Paris owned 5,772 lanterns of this type.

In 1745, oil replaced the candle, and reflectors were installed in the lamps. By 1769, they were in general use around Paris—no longer on the walls but on 15-foot poles situated every 200 feet along the streets. The number of lanterns increased regularly in the first years of the 19th century.

The first gas lamps appeared in 1829, installed along la rue de la Paix. By 1869, there were more than 23,000 throughout the city. Electricity came slowly. Introduced in 1920, it replaced the last gas lamps in the 1950s. Today there are 142,000 incandescent, fluorescent, and sodium lamps in Paris. In addition, there are 11,000 special lamps used to illuminate 155 monuments on occasion.

Some Background

Barbarian Paris—the Paris that remained after the collapse of Roman Gaul—has been described as "a violent country town of 10- or at the most 15-thousand souls. Rome had perished, how much of

2

Lutetia was still standing at this time is a matter for conjecture, probably more than is generally believed, but it must have been in very poor condition. For three-hundred years the Parisians had stripped Roman structures of all the useful stone that could conveniently be dragged away. Throughout the Dark Ages the beautifully tailored Roman material was torn from the buildings, was employed for every sort of construction project, for barns and sarcophagi, for fortresses and abbeys." (From *The History of the Franks*, by Gregory of Tours, translated by O.M. Dalton, Oxford University Press, 1927.)

Once Notre Dame was built, the city began to rise around it. Even earlier, though, Philippe Augustus, the first king to see the possibilities of Paris, had begun the process by ordering the four main streets of Paris to be paved with stones three-feet square and six-inches thick. (It wasn't until the mid-17th century that Paris was completely paved.)

Since then, Paris has gradually become the city we know today. The stockyards and abattoirs that once dotted the Paris map have all gone. The last and largest has become a gigantic museum of science and technology, another a public park (a statue of a great bull still bears witness to its former use). Some remaining street names suggest they once had or were near slaughterhouses: de la Tuerie (slaughter), de l'Ecarcherie (skinner), de la Triperie (tripe trade).

The public baths, a feature of the Paris scene as late as 1968 when only 30% of Paris homes had baths and only 20% had hot water, have now dwindled to almost none. Electric street lamps have finally replaced all the 19th-century gas lamps, and house numbers have replaced the old pictorial signs that once identified residences as well as commercial establishments.

Recent times, however, have seen an enormous surge in public building, beginning with the UNESCO building in 1955, the monument to Jewish martyrs in 1956, and in 1962 the memorial to *les déportés*. And there was la Maison de la Radio in 1957. At the end of the 1950s the city started a housing plan that resulted in 200,000 new living units. Among them were the first high-rises, which generated strong criticism. During this period, work began on an automobile belt highway circling the city and on a freeway along the Seine. In 1961, the suburban train system, the RER, was started.

The 1960s were marked by major university constructions: in 1961 the Curie Institute, in 1965 the Faculty of Science at Jussieu, in 1968 l'Hôpital Necker, and in 1969 la Maison des Sciences de l'Homme, the law school at la rue d'Assas, and l'Ecole Nationale des Arts Décoratifs.

In 1962 the government built a new museum of arts and popular traditions. And at the urging of Andre Malraux, the first campaign of

3

facade cleaning was begun in 1965. During the presidency of Pompidou (1969-1974), the decision was made to move the wholesale food market outside Paris; to tear down the historic iron and glass "umbrellas" designed by Baltard for Napoleon III; to build a motorway along the banks of the Seine, a high-rise and business complex in Montparnasse, and a cluster of 20-story apartments on the banks of the Seine; to Manhattanize the height west of Paris known as la Défense; to build university buildings (including one that looms over Notre Dame) in place of the ancient Paris wine market; to rebuild the entire neighborhood of la Porte d'Italie; to scoop out two score of underground parking lots beneath Paris streets; to rebuild la Porte Maillot with a gigantic convention hall and two high-rise hotels; and (to his credit) to create a center of modern art and house it in what may be the world's most modern building. Pompidou also wanted to tear down la Gare d'Orsay and replace it with a Hilton Hotel.

Fortunately, cooler heads prevailed. Giscard d'Estaing, who took office in 1974, stopped the skyscraper at la Porte d'Italie, saved la Gare d'Orsay, and generally modified the plan to "modernize" Paris.

Le Centre National d'Art et de Culture Georges Pompidou opened in January 1977 with immediate success. Within a year, the museum was attracting more people than la Tour Eiffel. Les Halles, Pompidou's 35-acre urban renewal project, has seen 17 years of excavation and filling in. Today it is almost complete. The last unfinished corner will contain an oceanographic center designed by Jean-Jacques Cousteau.

A magnificent town house in le Marais has been successfully converted into a Picasso museum for the works that fell into government hands as the inheritance tax on the artist's estate.

La Gare d'Orsay, on the Left Bank of the Seine across from the Louvre, has been converted from an unused railroad station into what promises to be one of the world's great museums of art and artifacts.

A modern slaughterhouse that was never used and that caused a major scandal in the 1960s has been transformed into a city of science and the area surrounding it into an appealing public park. More projects are under way. A pair of 30-story buildings connected across the top will provide the final touch on the new complex of high-rises on the height west of Paris known as la Défense. The buildings complete a line of sight that starts in the horseshoe court of le Louvre, goes the length of les Tuileries, crosses la Place de la Concorde, and goes up les Champs-Elysées, through l'Arc de Triomphe, and to the top of la Défense. This project, President François Mitterrand's bid for immortality, may be canceled by a new government before it is completed, however.

On July 14th, 1989, the 200th anniversary of the storming of la Bastille, Paris' new opera house will be inaugurated. (If funds hold out and the project does not meet with government opposition in the meantime.) The opera house is on la place de la Bastille.

The venerable Louvre, once home to French kings and since 1793 one of the finest museums of art in the world, is being drastically renovated. A new entrance will be covered with an ultra-modern, all-glass pyramid conspicuously placed in the center of le Cours Napoléon. The work, scheduled to be finished by the end of 1987, appears to be running six months to a year behind schedule. The French Ministry of Finance, which has occupied a wing of the Louvre since 1855, is scheduled to move to a new building on the bank of the Seine near la Gare de Lyon sometime this year.

Across the river, on the Left Bank at the site of the old wholesale wine market, two enormous connected buildings have been built. These are the Arab World Studies Center and the Museum of Arab Civilization and Art.

Not yet completed is a full-size Disneyland park in a nearby suburb of Paris. Jacques Chirac, the mayor of Paris, not to be outdone by predecessors, is talking about two huge buildings to be draped across the already dandied-up Porte Maillot. He is also considering a palace for water sports. Then, of course, there is the eternal possibility of a channel tunnel.

Le Café: a French Institution

Perhaps the most visible thing to an American his first time in Paris is the exterior life on the streets, notably the sidewalk café. Fifteen years ago Joseph Wechsburg wrote a most informative article in the *New York Times* on the subject. He made one mistake, however. The subhead of his article was, "The fading flower on the streets of Europe's capitals." Traditions, especially European traditions, do not die that easily. Wechsburg's reasoning was sensible—the fumes and noise from automobiles were driving people indoors. I guess two things have happened he did not count on: the proliferation of pedestrian streets and the ability of human beings to adapt.

I think it can safely be said that sidewalk *cafés* are here to stay. Since being introduced in France, they have served an immediate and important purpose. They give Frenchmen from every social strata a place to entertain or to be entertained. Living conditions in Paris through the ages were difficult even for the privileged and the intellectual. There was rarely space or comfort enough in homes to invite out-

5

siders, no matter how intimate. This has changed to a great extent, but *cafés* are still an important part of everyday life in the French capital.

It is in a *café* you meet someone before a movie or dinner. In a *café* you have coffee if you are on the run and have neither the time nor the urge to prepare it at home. In a *café* you rest your feet or find a toilet. In a *café* you wait for the rain to stop; you pick the numbers you will play in the lottery, or the horses you will bet to win. Students do their last bit of cramming here before an exam. In a *café* you can have a light lunch with a glass of good red wine, a drink, or coffee, while you check the items you just bought in a half-dozen shops. It is in a *café* in your neighborhood that you can find someone you know when you are lonely.

French Social Customs

Greetings are traditional, as are handshakes with just about anyone other than your concierge or waiter. Everyone gets a *"bonjour"* in the morning, a *"bonsoir"* in the evening. The change from *jour* to *soir* happens about noon. *"Bonne nuit"* is the final salutation before retiring for the night.

Politics, especially international policy, seldom affect personal loyalty, friendship, or relationships. No matter what the political climate between our two countries, Americans in France are usually accepted on an individual basis.

The French are well-read, and their reading is not confined to French writers. Some 2,867 books were translated into French from other languages in 1985; 71% of these were translated from English.

Who are the French?

It would be difficult to describe the typical French man or woman. The French are far too uncommon to be easily, much less casually, labeled. The best we can do is consider how a Frenchman knows a Frenchman. According to Sanche de Gramont (now known as Ted Morgan, an anagram of his French name) who was raised in France, "The Frenchman is not someone who possesses a navy blue passport and speaks the language of Descartes, but someone who knows who broke the Soissons vase, what happened to Buridan's donkey, why Parmentier gave his name to a hash, and why Charles Martel saved Christiandom." I find this to be a fair means of describing any national. An American, on the other hand, knows who chopped down the cherry tree.

Chapter II

Paris by Arrondissement

The 1st, 2nd, 3rd, and 4th *Arrondissements*

The four central *arrondissements* have been the nerve center of Paris for centuries. Today they are the hub of life on the Right Bank. Le Louvre, le Palais Royal, and la Place Vendôme are sparkling tourist attractions, well covered in the guides to Paris.

Le Forum des Halles, le Beaubourg, some of the little streets and neighborhoods, and le Marais are worth more consideration than they get in the standard guidebooks. It is these we will consider here.

Le Forum des Halles

Le Forum des Halles is too new for proper guidebook coverage. This massive project is on the site of the old Paris wholesale food market, les Halles. The market in this location dated from 1137, when Louis VI banned the market from operating in front of the city hall.

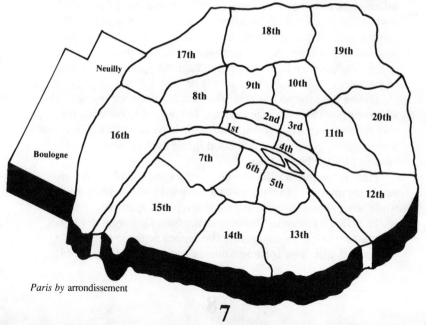

Paris by arrondissement

He created an official open-air merchandise market on le Champeaux, a meadow then outside Paris on the road to Saint Denis. Less than 50 years later two halls were built to house the drapers and weavers who had set up there. And King Saint-Louis added buildings for thread dealers, leather curriers, and fishmongers. By 1553, when King Henri II reconstructed les Halles, it was primarily a wholesale food market. In 1788, a vegetable hall was built on land taken from the nearby cemetery of the Church of the Innocents. During this time the quarter became the major commodity market and banking center of the city. By the 19th century, les Halles was so established a feature of Paris that even Napoléan III's Prefect of Paris, Georges Haussmann, allowed it to remain. Typically, he could not refrain from improving it and had glass and cast-iron umbrellas, designed by Baltard, erected to house the stalls.

But even les Halles couldn't survive the 20th century. In March 1969, in a single night, almost the entire market was closed and merchants moved to Rungis, a stretch of flat land on the road to Orly Airport. The butchers, originally scheduled to go to la Villette, remained at les Halles for a few months before moving to Rungis. For a year or more the deserted halls and their extensive cellars were used for theater, fairs, expositions, concerts, and playgrounds, creating an amusing quarter with character and a rich history.

Plans were drawn and approved for a complex that was to be an international commercial and convention center. In spite of public demonstrations and petitions, the historic halls were torn down. (One was saved and reconstructed in the suburb of Nogent-sur-Marne.) There followed the creation of a gaping, surrealistic hole more than six stories deep that remained for several years. It was so terrible a sight that it actually attracted tourists, and balconies were built as public observation platforms. A new metro station was put in, and two lines of the suburban train RER were run through the space at the bottom of the hole.

During this time no less than 10 architects succeeded one another with their plans to resuscitate the area. The request to construct the convention center was refused. Among the ideas that followed was one that suggested diverting the Seine and filling the hole with water to create a pleasure boat marina.

Finally, the hole was filled with corridors and chambers. An inverted pyramid full of shops, with the advantage of providing daylight while being almost invisible at ground level, was approved.

In 1978 a commercial shopping center called le Forum des Halles was the first unit to be completed. The surface began to take form a year or two later. Two apartment houses were built on la rue Turbigo (one served to hide one of the sheer cement walls of the ventilator that rose above the pyramid), and the fate of the rest of the surface was decided. The result may not be ideal, but at least it's simple. Parisians should count their blessings.

From the outside, the new Forum des Halles shares certain design elements with its forebearer. It consists of a half-dozen glittering aluminum and glass "umbrellas" not too unlike those torn down 20 years ago. They contain cultural houses of poetry, music, and dance and an excellent small art gallery.

At ground level are playgrounds, tree-lined walks, a semicircle of fieldstone facing the intriguing south facade of the Church of Saint Eustache, a gigantic sculpture, small streams and waterfalls, and three glass pyramids containing tropical plants and trees. There are a number of elaborate entrances to the underground complex of shopping malls, a swimming pool, a billiard parlor, movie theaters, restaurants, *cafés*, and a wax museum.

The small unfinished section will eventually become a museum of the sea. The museum, to be called le Centre Océanique, will be supervised by Jean-Jacques Cousteau and will cover an area of more than 90,000 square feet on three levels. For about the same entrance fee as a movie house (FF40) visitors will be introduced to the mysteries of the silent world: vast fields of algae, deep-sea creatures, and coral growths. Visitors will be able to explore the inside of a 75-foot whale, an experience presently exclusive to Jonah. And there will be animations, simulations, deep-sea scenes, and films made on expeditions of Cousteau's exploration boat *Calypso*.

Le Centre National d'Art et de Culture (CNAC)

"I want a museum like that one in New York," Georges Pompidou, president of France, is reported to have demanded. He was referring to New York's Museum of Modern Art, which at the time was probably unique in the world. Shortly after the Pompidou Center—as the CNAC is known—opened in January 1977, it became the number-one attraction for visitors to Paris. Built on the site of an 11th-century village called Beaubourg, the CNAC is also referred to simply as le Beaubourg. It contains six units.

Exploring the Quarters

There are many interesting old streets around les Halles and le Beaubourg. Take time to meander along la rue Saint-Honoré, le Marché-Saint-Honoré, la rue des Petits-Champs, la place des Victoires, and la place des Petits Pères. There are interesting arcades

9

on la rue des Petits-Champs: le Choiseul at number 42, le Colbert at number 6, and la Vivienne at number 4. The shortest street in Paris, actually a stairway of 14 steps, is la rue des Degrés running between la rue de Clery and la rue Beauregard (2nd *arrondissement*).

The history of *la place* and la Fontaine des Innocents is covered well in guidebooks. Today it is a pleasant spot to stop for a drink. Try le Café Costes at 45 rue Saint-Denis (la place des Innocents). There's another Café Costes at la rue Saint-Martin in front of le Beaubourg. At both the interior decoration is by Philippe Starck, who also designed the furniture. The result is quite sensational.

The nearby rue de la Ferronnerie came by its name because in 1229 King Saint-Louis authorized metalworkers to establish their forges along this street. Until then, it had been called la rue des Charrons. The assassination of King Henri IV occurred here in a 17th-century traffic jam.

An enjoyable way to see how Paris looked during *la Belle Epoque* is to visit le Musée Grévin. It's on the first level (*niveau* 1) of le Forum des Halles.

La Bibliothèque Nationale, 58 rue de Richelieu, often has interesting exhibits. Look at *Pariscope,* the weekly guide, to see what's going on. Part of *la bibliothèque* is the shopping arcade le Colbert, which has recently been renovated with splendid results. In it is a pleasant *café,* space for exhibits and concerts, the office where one registers a copyright for published works, and a small museum shop.

The 2nd *Arrondissement*

On the Right Bank, the wedge of Paris between la rue Etienne Marcel and *les grands boulevards* makes up the 2nd *arrondissement*. This is mostly a business quarter that empties out at night and weekends. The most important activity is la Bourse (stock market), followed by clothing manufacturers, fabric wholesalers, Paris' ready-to-wear, and newspaper publishers.

An interesting place is **le Quartier Sentier**, which gets its name from a simple deformation of the word *chanter* (to sing). Printers, engravers, and designers had workshops here before the days of neon light. They came because the low skyline allowed strong clear light and a maximum of daylight working hours. Today you can see many examples of pre-electric architecture—studios and print shops with glass and metal domes or skylights.

Along la rue Réaumur are examples of excellent late 19th-century commercial architecture. Modern technique and academic ideas (which included *Art Nouveau*) were combined here.

The 3rd *Arrondissement*

Les grands boulevards of Paris that run along the northern border of the 3rd *arrondissement* are described as part of the discussion of *arrondissements* 8 and 9. They have more to do with these later additions to Paris than the ancient neighborhoods of the 3rd.

For a taste of medieval Paris, walk la rue Française, la rue Tiquetonne, le Passage du Grand Cerf, and la rue Greneta. On la rue Française, la Tour Jean Sans Peur (early 15th century) is all that is left of **l'Hôtel de Bourgogne**, home of John the Fearless. John the Fearless would be remembered better if the plaque at 31 rue des Francs Bourgeois was still in its place. The missing plaque read, "...in this passage, an exit from l'Hôtel Barbette, Duke Louis of Orléans, brother of King Charles VI, was assassinated by John the Fearless, the duke of Bourgogne, during the night of 23 to 24 November, 1407."

The duke of Orléans had been dining with Queen Isabeau, his sister-in-law and probable mistress, at l'Hôtel Barbette, where she lived separated from her husband. A messenger arrived with a supposed summons to the king. Enroute to l'Hôtel Saint-Paul, the duke was attacked and murdered by hirelings of the duke of Bourgogne.

Duke John added a tower to his home, l'Hôtel de Bourgogne, for protection from Armagnac vengance. The hotel later became a theater where the great tragedies of Racine and Cornielle were first performed. The first act of the modern classic *Cyrano de Bergerac* by Rostand is set here. Today, only the tower remains.

Le Marais

Incorporating a large section of the 2nd and 3rd *arrondissements*, le Marais is one of the most interesting and beautiful parts of Paris. It is bounded by la rue Beaubourg on the west, le boulevard Beaumarchais on the east, the river on the south, and les rues Réaumur and Bretagne on the north. Within its confines are literally scores of fine old town houses, most built with a paved forecourt and a verdant walled garden in the rear. There are also several major museums: les Archives Nationales, le Quartier Juif, la place des Vosges, and a half-dozen interesting churches.

The name le Marais means "marshland" and originated early in the history of Paris when branches of the Seine in that area continually flooded. For centuries le Marais was shunned, while Paris grew to the south and the west. Then, in the late 13th century, the military-religious order the **Knights Templars** returned to Europe from the Holy Land. They built their headquarters in London and Paris. The

11

Paris temple was a typical five-story stone tower castle with little round turrets at each corner. Its only neighbor in the unpopular Marais was l'Abbaye de Saint-Martin on the road to Saint-Denis. The Knights, who had switched from crusading to banking and moneylending, were very rich. Within a short time they owned all le Marais. Not long after that they were abolished and their property confiscated by Philippe IV. The castle remained in the hands of their brother order, the Knights Hospitaliers, known as the Knights of Malta, until the 18th century. It was here that Louis XVI was held prisoner and his young son probably died.

Throughout the years, le Marais was drained, roads were built, and people began to move here. But it was not until the middle of the 14th century, when Charles V decided to move the palace east outside the walls of Philippe II, that le Marais became prosperous.

Charles V bought some large houses and built a palace complex in an area today bounded by les rues Saint-Antoine, Saint-Paul, and Petite-Muse (originally Pute-y-Muse). The compound was known as **l'Hôtel Saint-Paul** and was surrounded by a high wall. Within the wall were meadows, gardens, and even a small menagerie. Charles V built two churches, both of which disappeared at the time of the Revolution. The palace itself vanished in the 16th century. All that remains today is a little turret on the corner of les rues Saint-Paul and des Lions.

In the early 15th century, Paris was occupied by the English king Henry V. When he died, the Regent of Bedford, who ruled France for the infant son of Henry V, decided not to live in l'Hôtel Saint-Paul. He established his court in a 14th-century building near where la place des Vosges is located today.

Joan of Arc, like deGaulle 500 years later, refused to accept English rule. And, also like deGaulle, she did something about it. As a result, French kings resumed the rule of France. But for the rest of the century, they rarely—if ever—came to Paris.

Nevertheless, at the end of the 15th century, the rich, cultivated, and noble people of Paris discovered le Marais. It was a garden spot within the walls of Paris. Le Marais became the heart of Paris and continued in that role for nearly 200 years. Unfortunately, few of the grand old houses of that period remain. One exception is **la Bibliothèque de Fornay,** built from 1474 to 1514.

The 16th century's first two French kings, Louis XII and François I, did little for Paris, with one important exception. In the 1540s, François I built the incomparable **l'Hôtel Carnavalet**, one of the finer houses in le Marais and today the museum of the city of Paris.

The Pierre d'Orgemont house that had been occupied by Bedford was located on what is now the north side of la place des Vosges. It was a large and beautiful mansion with gardens enclosed in a wall decorated with a large number of little towers—from which it got its name, **l'Hôtel des Tournelles**. The estate became crown property in the 15th century and was enlarged into a complex much like that of l'Hôtel Saint-Paul. It had individual houses, chapels, and a commons, all connected by a dozen galleries with a cloister, *un preau* (playground) between two parks, six gardens, and several little woods and pastures. Today's rue du Foin (Hay Street) took its name from the path that led to one of the pastures.

Le Palais de Tournelles, as it was then called, was torn down as a result of an untimely death in 1559. King Henri II, concluding a week of celebrating a double royal marriage, insisted on a last joust with Count Montgomery, commander of the Scottish Guards. Somehow, Montgomery's broken lance forced open Henry's visor and a splinter entered through the eye into the brain. After several days of agony he died.

His wife, Queen Catherine de Médici, ordered the destruction of le Palais de Tournelles, where the tournament had taken place. The gardens were destroyed, the mansions and towered wall torn down, and the moats were filled. A horse market opened on the site, and the only relic of bygone splendors was in the street name, la rue des Tournelles.

In 1605, Henri IV decided to build on the site again. The horse market was already notorious as "une Cour des Miracles"—a hangout for thieves. Interested in the development of silk manufacturing and weaving, Henri wanted to set up an Italian silk works on the old Paris site. As the plan grew, however, he changed his mind. Instead of a silk works, the old horse market was to become a royal square with rows of uniform houses on all sides. The red-brick buildings were trimmed with white stone and had slate roofs. Apart from a few simple modifications of ironwork, la place des Vosges is still much as Henri envisioned it. (As Victor Hugo wrote, "It was the broken lance of Montgomery that created la place des Vosges.")

Henri IV did not live to move into the king's house on the south side of the square. He was murdered in 1610, and the square was still unfinished. When the work was completed two years later, the event was marked by a three-day equestrian ballet. The "Tourney of the Glorious Cavaliers" played to the music of 150 musicians and was punctuated by the sound of gunfire from the cannons of the Bastille.

La place Royale, as it was called then, brought new prosperity to le Marais, and for a time it became the commercial heart of Paris.

In 1682, however, the courtiers abandoned Paris for Versailles, and many of those who remained in town moved to the newly fashionable faubourg-Saint-Germain. Le Marais was virtually abandoned once again.

But not for long. It regained popularity during the 18th century, when *salons* became fashionable, and the grand houses were reopened to become the cultural and spiritual centers of France.

When the Bastille fell in 1789, le Marais saw another reversal in fortune. The houses emptied as the royal and rich either disappeared or were executed. La place Royale was renamed la place des Fédérés and then la place de l'Indivisibilité. The square first took the name la place des Vosges in 1800 to honor the first *département* to discharge its liabilities for the Revolutionary War.

By the end of the Revolution, the entire quarter was virtually abandoned. In the years

La place de la Bastille.

that followed, squatters, businessmen, artisans, and small manufacturers filled the majestic houses, using them as warehouses, factories, or ateliers. Almost none were occupied as living quarters. Le Marais remained in this declining state until 1962 when André Malraux, then deGaulle's minister of culture, classed the entire area as a historic monument. Since then le Marais has been gradually restored to its 18th-century grandeur.

The Cradle of Paris: the 4th *Arrondissement*

L'Ile de la Cité in the 4th *arrondissement* is where Paris began. The prehistoric Celtic tribe Parisii settled here, where they had the wide, swift Seine between them and potential enemies. The Roman conquerors of ancient Gaul found the island a bit too damp, and they settled on the Left Bank of the river. It is now known as **le Quartier**

Latin. When the first French kings chose Paris as the/ ever, they built their castles on the river's island.

To see what Paris was like then, visit **la Crypte logique** (Archaeological Crypt) under *le parvis* (square) ơi і. Dame. Walk the little narrow streets near the cathedral: la rue de la Colombe, la rue Chanoinesse, la rue des Chantres, and la rue des Ursins.

Quite the opposite of l'Ile de la Cité, **l'Ile Saint-Louis** was created by a 17th-century real estate promotion combining the islands of l'Ile des Vaches (Cow Island, probably because cattle grazed there) and l'Ile de Notre Dame. The neighborhood is now very chic. There is almost a complete lack of city transportation available to residents or visitors, however.

Recommended Restaurants

Michelin publishes the annual red guide for Paris restaurants and hotels. It costs FF11 ($1.85). This is, hands down, the best restaurant guide for Paris. Unfortunately, the *Michelin* invariably quotes prices a bit below actual costs, so add 10% for a more accurate estimate. Of the other guidebooks, the *Gault-Millau Paris* is the easiest to use and is essential for anyone living in the city.

Most restaurants listed below appear in one guide or another. There are very few restaurants worth listing that are not already mentioned in a guide; however, we have included a few in our list below. *All prices are per person.*

Mercure Galant, 15 rue des Petits-Champs, 1st; tel. 42.97.53.85. Closed Saturday for lunch and Sunday. One star from *Michelin*. Everything here is good, and the service matches the food. FF350 or more.

Chez Pauline, 5 rue Villedo, 1st; tel. 42.96.20.70. Closed Saturday evening and Sunday. Open for more than 30 years, this restaurant has always enjoyed a good reputation. *Michelin* gives it one star. Handed down from father to son, it has remained first-class and is one of the few restaurants in France where one can have a soup called *Billy By* that is made with cream and mussels. In the autumn many dishes feature wild mushrooms and game. A good choice of Beaujolais wines is available and a selection from the Rhone as well. At least FF300 or a bit more.

Le Cochon d'Or, 31 rue du Jour, 1st; tel. 42.36.38.31. Closed Saturday for lunch and Sunday. This is a very old restaurant with a new chef but thankfully not *nouvelle cuisine*. More than FF300.

L'Epi d'Or, 25 rue Jean-Jacques Rousseau, 1st; tel. 42.36.38.

.2. Closed Sunday. Not in any guidebook that I know of. This is a perfectly fine restaurant for the price. Less than FF200.

Pharamond, 24 rue Grande-Truanderie, 1st; tel. 42.33.06.72 0672. Closed Sunday, Monday for lunch, and July. The food, like the decor, is authentic. If you want to try *les tripes á la mode de Caen*, this is the place. The tripe is served in a pot over glowing coals and cannot be beat in Paris. *Les pommes de terre soufflées* are worth the price of the meal. The restaurant has been in all the guidebooks for more than a half-century. More than FF200.

Au Pied de Cochon, 6 rue Coquillière, 1st; tel. 42.36.11.75. Open 24 hours a day year-round. A bit of charm for about FF250 a person.

Pierre Traiteur, 10 rue de Richelieu, 1st; tel. 42.96.09.17. This restaurant gained a reputation during the 1930s, maintained it, and passed it along to the son who carried on with high marks. It has been sold, and we hope it will continue to be good. *Le foie gras*, green cabbage salad with bacon, sausage (*Jésu de Morteau*) poached in Beaujolais, roast saddle of lamb with *les gratins dauphinois* (sliced potatoes baked in stock and sprinkled with cheese), *le boeuf á la ficelle* (beef dipped in boiling stock before roasting), lamb stew, roast pigeon with garlic, *la poule au pot* (chicken). It was all good, costing about FF300.

Chez la Vielle, 37 rue de l'Arbre Sec, 1st; tel. 42.60.15.78. Lunch only; closed Saturday and Sunday. Madame Biasin is *la Vieille,* although she is not at all *vieille.* Her food, however, is fine old-fashioned back-burner cooking, including *le navarin d'agneau* (lamb stew), *le gigot hérissé d'ail* (leg of lamb with garlic), and *la fricassée de canard au vinaigre de cidre au Saint-Raphael blanc* (in two words, duck stew, but it would take several pages to describe eating it). No frills, just plain good food. It's hard to get in, and your best bet is during school holidays when her regular customers are away from Paris. Don't go without a reservation, you will find a *complet* (full) sign on the door. Close to FF300.

Robert Vattier, 14 rue Coquillière, 1st; tel. 42.36.51.60. Not in any guidebook but the nearest thing to one of the old les Halles restaurants that is left. The seafood plate is as good as at the restaurant next to it—and considerably less expensive. Figure FF200.

Chez Georges, 1 rue du Mail, 2nd; tel. 42.60.07.11. Closed Sunday. Traditional is the word for Georges. No great back-burner dishes, but everything as it should be. He appears to have been here for a generation, but actually it's been only about 15 years. No less than FF200.

Gerard, 4 rue du Mail, 2nd; tel. 42.96.24.36. Closed Sunday.

This is a hang-out for actors and theater-goers, not to see and but to eat. No teenagers. Good solid dishes such as *le pot-au-feu* (boiled beef). Probably a bit more than FF200.

Chez Pierrot, 18 rue Etienne Marcel, 1st; tel. 45.08.17.64. Closed Saturday and Sunday. The telephone number of this good little restaurant is the same as one in an old les Halles *bistrot*. Pierrot, who worked in that restaurant (which disappeared with the old market), kept the number when he opened his own place about 15 years ago. His *hors-d'oeuvres* are displayed on a table (there are at least a dozen) and brought to you just as they did in the original restaurant. Good main courses, especially beef. Light Beaujolais and white wines of the Loire Valley are the specialty. About FF200.

Vaudeville, 29 rue Vivienne, 1st; tel. 42.33.39.31. One of four *brasseries* owned by Monsieur Bucher. Like the others, it is noisy and fun and has good food. An excellent supply of oysters and crustaceans all summer long. Reisling by the pitcher. Wonderful 1920s decor on the site of the theater where *La Dame des Camélias* made its debut. Across from la Bourse, the French stock market. About FF200.

Brisse-Moret, 5 rue Saint-Marc, 2nd; tel. 42.36.91.72. Not in any guide, but it should be. Inexpensive but excellent food. A strange ambiance—certainly not "redone" but not "done" either. An unusual place, but nice. Directly behind la Bourse. Less than FF100.

Brasserie Gus, 157 rue Montmartre, 1st; tel. 42.36.68.40. Open only for lunch except Friday, when dinner is served. There are a lot of imitation *fin de siècle brasseries* in Paris, but this one is authentic. One of the best and least expensive. A little more than FF100.

Le Pistou de Fernand, 29 rue Tiquetonne, 2nd; tel. 42.61.94.85. Closed Sunday. Fernand moved from the Left Bank to this location. A very small place with several very nice dishes, including *le cassoulet périgourdin, le carré d'agneau* (lamb) with wild mushrooms, and jellied rabbit. Just more than FF100.

Ambassade d'Auvergne, 22 rue du Grenier-Saint Lazare, 3rd; tel. 42.72.31.22. Closed Sunday. Exactly what its name suggests, this restaurant is owned by a gastronomic ambassador from the Auvergne region of France. In all the guidebooks. The cooking is something very special and do not miss *l'aligot*, a sort of mashed potatoes with cheese. About FF250.

Le Petit Prieuré, 6 rue Elevir, 3rd; tel. 42.72.77.59. Not in any guidebook—and with reason, for the food is nothing special. But this restaurant is comfortable and handy to the Carnavalet and the Picasso museums. Not expensive, FF100 or less.

La Calanque, 2 rue de la Coutellerie, 4th; tel. 42.72.34.21. Closed Saturday and Sunday. Not in the guides, but you can get *la*

17

bouillabaisse here. About FF150.

Benoît, 20 rue Saint-Martin, 4th; tel. 42.72.25.76. Closed Saturday and Sunday. This venerable establishment opened its doors in 1912 and has been in all the guides since. (*Michelin* gives it one star.) The present patron, Michel Petit, is the grandson of Benoît Matray, who opened the restaurant. This is what might be called *bourgeoise* and Lyonnaise cooking. Typical dishes, such as *le saucisson chaud* (hot Lyonnais sausage), *le boudin* (blood sausage) house-made with potatoes and apples, veal tongue with a vinaigrette and herb sauce, and roast duck with turnips. About FF300.

Bofinger, 5 rue de la Bastille, 4th; tel. 42.72.87.82. One of the most beautiful *brasseries* in a town full of beautiful *brasseries*. Good atmosphere, good food, and very fair prices. In all the guidebooks. Up to FF220.

Coconnas, 2*bis* place des Vosges, 4th; tel. 42.78.58.16. A beautiful restaurant in one of the most beautiful squares in Paris. This is the best of several restaurants around the place. The menu changes often, but it's always good. Nice terrace for summer dining under the arcades. Figure close to FF300.

Chez Rabu, 10 rue des Haudriettes, 3rd; tel. 42.72.10.43. Lunches only, closed on Sunday. When you see Madame Rabu going from table to table you somehow feel sure all is well in the kitchen, otherwise she would be in there. A typical French *café* bill of fare with such classics as *moules á la crème* and *omelette au lard* for starters, *navarin de mouton* (mutton), *foie de veau* (calves liver), or *cervelles* (brains) for a main course, and a glass of calvados (FF20) to finish the meal. A bit more than FF100, with the calvados.

The latest development in le Marais is the appearance of very small inexpensive restaurants with simple menus, operated for the most part by young people. These are not bad, but they are not the traditional French way to eat, nor do they serve traditional food.

The 5th, 6th, and 7th *Arrondissements*

These three *arrondissements* compose the famous Rive Gauche (the Left Bank of the Seine) in the center of Paris. Very different from each other, each of these *arrondissement* represents a different period of Paris history.

The Fifth *Arrondissement*

The 5th is where the Romans, 50 years before Christ, moved the town to its "damp" island. Emperor Julian spent the winter of A.D.

357-358 "In our beloved Lutetia, for so the Gauls term the little town of the Parisii...." On the Left Bank of the river the Romans built their thermal baths, an arena, a theater, and other public buildings on what became known as la Montagne Sainte Genevieve. The hill was named for the patron saint of Paris. What's now la rue Saint Jacques was the Roman road to the south.

The University of Paris

In the beginning of the 12th century, Abailard left the cloisters of Notre Dame to give his lessons away from the bishop's influence. He took with him the best students, and at the foot of la Montagne Genevieve began new courses taught by liberal masters. This university of professors and students was granted special privileges by King Philippe Auguste. For a long time the university was a state within a state. But without financial resources Abailard was unable to provide lodgings or classrooms. Rich benefactors came to the rescue by founding **les collèges.**

The first *collèges* date from the end of the reign of Louis VII (1180). At that time these charitable foundations provided only modest quarters and scholarships. Lectures were given outdoors at la place Maubert and la rue Fouarre. Students gathered in the early morning and sat on the ground or on bales of hay (the haymarket was at la rue Fouarre).

Les grands collèges gave classes on all branches of learning, while the more numerous **les petits collèges** offered only one subject. Most colleges took the names of their benefactors—for example, le Collège d'Harcourt and le Collège du Cardinal-Lemoine.

In all colleges, everyone (the principal, professors, students, and servants) spoke only Latin, both in and out of class. Although Latin was spoken only until the Revolution, the name le Quartier Latin remained.

In 1792, following the Revolution, l'Université de Paris and the 17 provincial universities were discontinued. It wasn't until 1806 that the Emperor Napoléon re-established them. The University of France exists today pretty much as it was set up then.

Old Streets

Between the river and le boulevard Saint-Germain, many of the narrow twisting streets are typical of medieval Paris. Walk la rue Mâitre Albert to la place Maubert, where Mâitre Albert, a 12th-century Dominican savant, held his classes. La rue de la Bucherie and the

19

streets around the Church of Saint-Sèverin are named mostly after the shops that were located on them. Shop signs were one of the greatest contributors to street names. **La rue Parcheminerie**, for example, was la rue des Ecrivains in the 13th century, because scribes were established here. When an enterprising parchment peddler moved into the street with a large sign over his shop, the street became known as la rue de la Parcheminerie.

On la rue Saint-Jacques, after you cross la rue Gay Lussac, is **le Val de Grâce**, a hospital built in the 17th century as an abbey for the Benedictine religious order. Across from le Val de Grâce at 1 rue du Val de Grâce and la rue Saint-Jacques is a little gastronomic and oenologic bookstore and gift shop. Called **le Verre et l'Assiette**, it's fun to visit.

La place de la Contrescarpe and the old market street called **la rue Mouffetard**, which leads into it, have a reputation for old-world charm. But *la place,* a pleasant, tree-lined square, has become a bit too polished, and the street borders on being cute. This is a far cry from its origin—the name Mouffetard, known since 1254, comes from *moffettes*, a disagreeable smell. The tripe shops and leather tanneries that once occupied the street undoubtedly inspired the name.

A few of the quaint shop signs still swing over la rue Mouffetard. One hangs over **le Café Bois & Charbon** at number 108. In the days when Paris apartments were heated by little coal stoves or fireplaces, there were many such *cafés*. They sold bundles of wood, bags of coal, and charcoal, and each had a small bar, usually with very inexpensive wines, aperitifs, and, oddly enough, a good calvados (not a popular drink in those days). There are a few such *cafés* left in Paris, but they become more rare each year.

In 1635 Louis XIII's physician established a garden of medicinal herbs. Throughout the years, it has grown into the huge botanical garden and zoo now known as **le Jardin des Plantes.** Today it contains a major laboratory for the study of plant life. There is also a menagerie, a winter garden, a botany school, and a museum of natural history.

Behind le Jardin des Plantes, on la place Puits-de-l'Ermite (so called after a 16th-century tanner named Adam l'Hermite who lived on the square), there is an imposing white mosque, built in 1926, with a minaret and a tea room. Another monument to the Middle East is at the top of le boulevard Saint-Germain on le Quai Saint-Bernard. There the new 10-story **Arab World Institute** reflects Notre Dame in its 270,000 square feet of double glass walls. Completed at the beginning of 1987, this mammoth addition to the Paris scene is built over part of the site of 17th-century wine halls. L'Université de Paris covers the rest of the site with massive buildings and a square tower piercing the horizon behind Notre Dame.

Along le Quai Saint-Bernard on the river front, a strip of land was once destined to be converted into a six-lane speedway. When that builder of superhighways and skyscrapers Georges Pompidou died, the project stopped. Instead, the space was converted into a quiet strolling park and an outdoor museum of contemporary statuary.

The 6th *Arrondissement*

Publishing is the principal industry in the 6th *arrondissement*, with more than 100 publishers in the quarter. Bookshops and literary *cafés* abound. The 6th likes to be thought of as intellectual. There is not much about this quarter that is not in the guidebooks; it has no secrets, no mysterious corners, no skeletons in the closet.

Its center point is the oldest church in Paris, **le Saint-Germain-des-Prés**, a 12th-century abbey built "in-the-fields" outside the walls of Paris (thus the name). The medieval abbey was virtually self-sufficient. Surrounded by walls and a moat, it housed its own bakers, butchers, and other providers and even had its own law courts and defense force. All that exists of this today, aside from the church, are the names of streets that refer to parts of the ancient abbey. Probably the wealthiest and most powerful of the abbeys in the Paris region at that time, it owned all the land for a considerable distance west of the present church and between what is now le boulevard Saint-Germain

The Luxembourg Gardens.

21

and the river. Today the abbey precincts are a quarter of small hotels, antique shops, rare bookstores, and l'Ecole des Beaux-Arts.

The literary *cafés* **le Flore** and **les Deux Magots** are across from the church on le boulevard Saint-Germain.

An Early Morning Outing *Do This*

Few visitors take advantage of the beautiful **Jardin du Luxembourg** at its best—in the early hours of the morning. If your hotel is in the neighborhood and you are *matinal* (a morning person), take a brisk morning walk through this public garden. At that hour it attracts a small army of panting and grunting joggers. But despite this distraction, the early morning sunshine filtering through the trees and mist can be awe-inspiring. And when the sky is overcast, shifting fog creates an aura of mystery. Afterward have coffee and a croissant at le Café de la Mairie in the square in front of Saint-Sulpice.

During the summer months in le Jardin du Luxembourg, there are some splendid palms and oleanders around the fountain. In the winter this tropical vegetation is moved inside to *une orangerie* just behind the museum near the west end of the garden. In summer, this indoor space is used as an exhibit hall, often for contemporary artists.

At the other end of the garden, also on la rue Guynemer side, is an experimental fruit farm and an apiary. The trees, magnificently kept and espaliered, produce some beautiful pears and apples. In late September or early October *l'orangerie* displays the products of the experimental gardens.

Ancient Landmarks

Between le Jardin du Luxembourg and le boulevard Saint-Germain is the Church of Saint-Sulpice. Originally built as a parish church for the abbey, Saint-Sulpice was rebuilt several times before Anne of Austria, widow of Louis XIII, laid the cornerstone of the present church in 1646. It was almost a century later, however, before the exterior was completed.

The square in front of Saint-Sulpice was completely redone in the 1970s when a parking lot was built underneath. The present chestnut trees replaced much older ones, but the new trees, like the old, bloom with pink, not white, blossoms. The fountain is a pleasant sight during the day as well as when it is illuminated at night.

On la rue Vaugirard, which borders le Jardin du Luxembourg on the north, and across from the Senate, is a row of recently reconstructed buildings. These belong to the Senate and are an interesting

example of 20th-century restoration. The arched stonework is i
cable, and the display windows along the sidewalk under the a
filled with examples of the gifts available in the various national
museum shops.

Between the buildings is la rue Garancière. The name comes from
an establishment called l'Hôtel de la Garancière; in ancient times *á la
garance* referred to a dye extracted from the roots of a flower. The street
leads to la rue Mabillon, where you will find le Marché Saint-
Germain, a covered market built in 1818 on the site of the last trace of
the Foire Saint-Germain, a commercial fair created by Louis XI in
1482. The merchants are now in a modern building, and most of the
old *marché* has been temporarily dismantled. On the streets on either
side of the decimated market (la rue Lobineau and la rue Clement), you
can see the beautiful timber rafters that held the roof above the two
lines of stone arches.

The south side of the square in front of the venerable Church of
Saint-Germain-des-Prés has recently had a change of name. It is now
la place de Quebec. The Canadian city of Quebec has donated an amusing fountain. Large blocks of the fieldstone paving appear to be erupt-
ing. Underneath, a dozen or more jets of water shoot foamy white
fountains just high enough to be seen through the displaced paving
but not high enough to overflow.

The nearby **Carrefour de la Croix-Rouge** was called le Carrefour de la Maladrerie (Leper House, after a neighboring hospital for
lepers) in the 15th century. It acquired its present name in the early
16th century when a cross painted in red marked the danger of contam-
ination. The cross and the hospital were removed in 1650 and eventually the name was changed to le Carrefour au Four. During the
Revolution, it temporarily acquired the name le Bonnet Rouge (Red
Cap).

There are three fine *cafés* in the immediate area of *le carrefour*. All
specialize in sourdough bread sandwiches and serve excellent beaujolais. Le Sauvignon at 80 rue des Saints-Pères (corner of la rue de
Sèvres) serves exceptional wine and tiny open sandwiches of Auvergnat ham, cheese, or pâté. Monsieur and Madame Vergne, and more
recently their daughter and her husband, have been pleasing people of
the neighborhood for more than 30 years. Finding a table here at noon
is difficult any day of the year. Farther along la rue de Sèvres at 2
Carrefour de la Croix Rouge is le Café Croix Rouge, where you can
get toasted Poilane bread with thin, rare slices of beef and a spicy mayonnaise that is sensational. Ask for *un Saint-Germain*. A bit farther
along, the street becomes la rue du Four. At number 54, le Tabac des
Sports also has a good choice of light and pleasant luncheons.

Les thermes, *or thermal baths.*

Going Under

It is a little-known fact that below the streets in this neighborhood
there are many caves and underground galleries. These are also found
in the 13th and 14th *arrondissements.* At various times in history,
stone, clay, and plaster have been commercially mined from Paris
soil. Stone for the earliest city buildings was taken from underground
and open-pit quarries located in what were then the suburbs of Paris.
Les thermes, or thermal baths, built during the Roman occupation,
the churches of Saint-Germain-des-Prés, Notre Dame, Saint-Julian-le-
Pauvre, and Saint-Sèverin, and many other structures up to the middle
of the 14th century were built with stone from beneath central Paris.

These subterranean mines have figured in the defense of Paris on
several occasions. In 1814 rumor had it that the Parisians had mined
the underground galleries and were prepared to blow up a part of Paris
should it be occupied. In 1870 the rumor was that the Prussians had
mined them and were ready to destroy the city. During the 1940-1944
Occupation, the Germans were said to have sheltered the air force headquarters under le Palais de Luxembourg and to have installed a telephone system. In 1944 the resistance installed two command posts in
the caves.

The little streets off **la rue Vavin** between la rue d'Assas and le
boulevard Montparnasse make a nice stroll, lined with interesting

shops, food stores, and examples of 1920s architecture. Follow either la rue d'Assas or la rue Notre-Dame-des-Champs to la place Camille-Jullian for a look at the extraordinary turtle fountain at the top of le Jardin du Luxembourg. **La Closerie des Lilas** is also close at hand (171 blvd. Montparnasse). This is the very last of many outdoor dance and pleasure halls that lined le boulevard Montparnasse in the late 19th century. The food is a bit overpriced (FF300 in the restaurant, less in the bar), and the service in the bar hits a true low for Paris. Yes, there are name plaques of famous writers on the tables, but one does not really believe them (although Hemingway does mention writing here).

The 7th *Arrondissement*

In addition to such tourist attractions as la Tour Eiffel and les Invalides, the 7th has many interesting streets lined with beautiful mansions and high-walled gardens. Most of these were built just before the Revolution when, in the late 18th century, the nobles and courtiers moved from le Marais to the part of the 7th known as le faubourg Saint-Germain.

Today most of these noble old town houses are occupied either by embassies (there are 16 in the 7th) or important government offices.

The name of **la rue des Saints-Pères,** where the 7th begins, is a deformation of Saint-Pierre, a 13th-century chapel that stood where the Saints-Pères crosses le boulevard Saint-Germain. Today the site is occupied by an 18th-century church used by Ukrainian Catholics.

As in the 6th, the streets between the river and le boulevard Saint-Germain (between la rue du Bac and la rue des Saints-Pères) are lined with elegant small antique shops. This whole section calls itself **les Antiquaires du Carré Rive Gauche** (Antique Dealers of the Left Bank Square).

Every spring, the shops decorate their windows with special artifacts, according to a preselected theme. Les Cinq Jours des Objets Extraordinaires (The Five Days of Extraordinary Objects) creates the mood of a fair. The objects are, as a rule, truly extraordinary.

La rue du Bac runs from the river to la rue de Sèvres. *Un bac,* or ferry, used to ply between the Left Bank and les Tuileries until the bridge was built in 1632.

At 140 rue du Bac, next to the department store Bon Marché, a high wooden door leads into an alley. Most of the inhabitants of Paris, including those who live in the 7th *arrondissement,* do not

25

know where it leads. But one-and-a-half-million Catholics visit a simple chapel at the back of the court every year.

The chapel commemorates Catherine Laboure, a 24-year-old novice of the order of the Sisters of Saint-Vincent-de-Paul. In November 1830, she swore she had received the following message: "Cast a medal to this model. Those who will carry it in faith will be blessed."

The medal was made with the approval of the archbishop of Paris, and thousands were sold. It is said that the young girl's vision and the medal of la rue du Bac miraculously resemble the features of *la dame de la grotte,* the vison seen by Bernadette. Bernadette was wearing a rue du Bac medal when she had her vision.

The Christian marvel of Sister Laboure was further confirmed when her body was exhumed in 1933 and was found to be intact: her eyes were blue, her limbs were supple. Dressed in the famous white habit of the Sisters of Charity, this saint can be seen today in la rue du Bac chapel.

The chaplain of the site, Father Brohan, receives several hundred letters a week, many including thanks for the benefits received as a result of a pilgrimage. There is such a demand for the miraculous medal that a slot machine has been installed in the chapel. When three five-franc pieces are put in the slot, the machine discharges a medal.

La rue de Bellechasse was constructed in 1085. It went through the enclosure of the convent of les Dames de Bellechasse. These nuns were part of an Augustinian sect of Saint-Sepulchre, founded in Palestine at the end of the 11th century.

At the river end of la Bellechasse is the magnificent old railroad station la Gare d'Orsay, now le Musée d'Orsay. It is a museum of arts and artifacts from the middle of the 19th century through the early years of the 20th century. The fabulous collection of Impressionist paintings, hung in le Jeu de Paume museum since 1947, was moved into the new museum, along with many other prints, sculptures, and artifacts. The new museum is a part of the Louvre.

One of the old 7th *arrondissement* mansions, **le Palais Bourbon,** has been refaced. In 1807, Napoléon ordered classic pillars to be put on the rear of *le palais* to match the classic style of the Madeleine church across the river. Today *le palais* is the National Assembly.

The 7th *arrondissement* is divided almost squarely in half by the esplanade of les Invalides, les Invalides itself, and the broad, tree-lined avenue de Breteuil.

To the west lies another residential neighborhood that is neither as old nor as elegant as those in the eastern half. One of the more interesting aspects of the western section, however, is the role it has played in nine Paris expositions since 1851.

La Tour Eiffel from the Exposition of 1889 is the most obvious trace of these world's fairs. Just across the river from la Tour Eiffel are **le Grand Palais** and **le Petit Palais**, built for the 1900 World Exhibition, and **le Palais de Chaillot** and **le Palais de Tokyo**, built for the 1937 World's Fair. On l'avenue Suffren is the **Swiss Village**, now a sophisticated antiques market. The **Pagode movie house** is on la rue de Babylone, and la Fontaine de Mars is on la rue Saint-Dominique.

The Grenelle Plain

The **Grenelle Plain,** the flat stretch of land running west to le Champs de Mars, was populated in the early 19th century as l'Ecole Militaire and les Invalides were being built. There is little here to attract a Paris visitor aside from some nice little restaurants, a pleasant market street (on la rue Cler), and the neat, architecturally satisfying rows of houses. At one time, the area was marshy farmland belonging mostly to the wealthy Abbey Saint-Germain. The rest was part of l'Abbaye Saint-Genevieve. The dividing point between these two properties was marked by a huge boulder known as *le Gros Caillou* (Big Stone), situated where la rue Cler and la rue Saint-Dominique meet today.

As building began on les Invalides and l'Ecole Militaire, the village le Bourg-du-Gros-Caillou grew around *le Gros Caillou.* In 1738 *le caillou* was destroyed by a considerable amount of explosives. But the name lived on, mainly because it was also the name of a very popular house of prostitution. A small street off la rue de Grenelle is still called le Gros Caillou.

The 1960s metamorphosis of Paris created a cluster of high-rise apartment houses and commercial buildings of bizarre design along the banks of the Seine on the Grenelle Plain. Officially called **le Front de Seine,** unofficially it is *l'Affront de Seine.*

The Grenelle Plain does have a few redeeming features, of course. Long before the current vogue for wine bars hit Paris, there was (and still is) an authentic wine bar here. **Le Sancerre** at 22 ave. Rapp is where Monsieur Guillaume serves white, rosé, and red wines from a number of communes of the Sancerre region. You can also order up terrines, omelets, ham, and goat cheese.

At 29 ave. Rapp is an exuberant *art nouveau* building designed by Jules Livirotte. Nearby in la place Rapp, the same architect designed a trompe-l'oeil latticework on a wall. Not far, at 10 rue Camou, is the **American Library**. It has a shelf of paperbacks available to anyone who will replace what he takes with another book. It's a good way to replenish your supply.

Recommended Restaurants

Chez Allard, 41 rue Saint-André des Arts, 6th; tel. 43.26.40. 23. Closed Saturday, Sunday, and August. Sometime back in the 1930s Madame Allard and her husband came to Paris and set up this restaurant. When they retired, their son and his wife carried on. For more than 50 years this family has demonstrated the glory of simple bourgeois French cuisine. After the second Monsieur Allard died, Madame chose to retire. Today the staff tries—and tries hard—to maintain the quality of a serious woman at a stove. They almost succeed and probably will do fairly well as long as Fernande Allard is around to supervise. This modest little restaurant held a prestigous two-star *Michelin* rating for almost 20 years. About FF300.

Les Arêtes, 165 blvd. du Montparnasse, 6th; tel. 43.26.23.98. Closed Saturday for lunch and Monday. The name of this place translates to "fishbones," but the rest of the fish is the good news here. The excellent fish dishes are reasonably priced at about FF250.

Atelier Maître Albert, 1 rue Maître Albert, 5th; tel. 46.33. 13.78. Dinner only; closed Sunday. A place of good taste and discretion—and that applies to the food as well as the atmosphere. More than FF200.

Balzar, 49 rue des Ecoles; tel. 43.54.13.64. Closed Tuesday and August. Balzar is one of the best *brasseries* in Paris and a wonderfully pleasant place to dine well.

Bistrot de la Grille, 1 rue Guisarde, 6th; tel. 43.54.16.87. Closed Sunday. Good food dispensed with dispatch and good humor. Young sophisticates eat here. About FF100 for lunch, a bit more for dinner.

Bistrot d'Henri, 15 rue Princesse; tel. 46.33.51.12. Henri is a young man who obviously loves good food. His tiny place (10 tables) is always full of young successful Parisians. His menu is fixed: a choice of four or five entrées followed by a plate of good hearty food (*le gigot*—mutton, *le rognon de veau*—calf's kidney, steak, calf's liver) that is always served with *les pommes de terre dauphinoise*—sliced potatoes cooked in stock and sprinkled with cheese, a dish that will make your day. The price is fixed—with wine it costs about FF150.

Henri has another place. **Le Machon d'Henri** is around the corner from *le bistrot* on la rue Guisarde. A good glass of wine served with sausages or cheese costs about FF80.

La Chope d'Orsay, 10 rue du Bac, 7th; tel. 42.61.21.89. Closed Saturday and Sunday. Elegant without being *snob,* it is best described as comfortable. The specialties include *boeuf á la ficelle* and *poulet á l'estragon.* FF220.

Dominique, 19 rue Brea, 6th; tel. 43.27.08.80. Closed July.
This is one of the very few non-French restaurants on my list. It is
Russian but has been a part of Montparnasse life for many years.
Borsch, blinis, smoked salmon, and beef strogonoff are served.
Dominique can be expensive, but when sitting at one of the counters
to eat blinis and drink a small vodka, one can get out for FF200.

l'Ecluse, 15 Quai des Grands Augustins, 6th; tel. 46.33.58.74.
One of the new arrivals to the Paris scene is the wine bar. There are a
lot of them, but the five or six called l'Ecluse are the best. The formula is wine by the glass, carafe, or bottle (very good, very expensive), with a snack or a platter of warm food. The snacks include
Dolomite ham, *le foie gras,* goat cheese, and warm plates such as
breast of potted duck. Only Bordeaux wine (quite expensive) is served.

Aux Fin Gourmets, 213 blvd. Saint-Germain, 5th; tel. 42.22.
06.57. Closed Saturday and August. This little place claims to be of
le Bearne, and most of the things it serves do come from that part of
France. *Le gigot* is excellent for the price. A nice Bearnese Irouleguy
wine. FF150.

Fontaine de Mars, 129 rue Sainte-Dominique, 7th; tel. 47.05.
46.44. Closed Saturday evening, Sunday, and August. Monsieur and
Madame Launay have run this delightful little neighborhood restaurant
for more than 25 years. It remains one of those simple restaurants that
demonstrates the greatness of French food. *La carte* changes with the
day and time of year, but if you are lucky you'll be here on a day they
are serving *le cassoulet au canard.* As the Launays are from the southwest of France, the house wine is Cahors. About FF100.

La Foux, 2 rue Clement, 6th; tel. 43.25.77.66. Closed Sunday.
Alex Guini, the chef/patron of la Foux, lived in Lyon as a boy and in
Nice as a student and studied the cuisines of both areas. His *carte* is
delicately balanced with specialties of both places. Each day he has *un
plat de jour,* and they are all good. On Saturday afternoon he gives his
restaurant the ambiance of *un bistrot*—le *menu* is on a blackboard, and
there are tumblers and *un pot de vin,* brown- and white-checked oil-
cloth on the tables, and aproned servers. In the summer months, Alex
creates a classic Nicoise *bistrot* with *pissalardière* (a sort of pizza with
onions, anchovies, and those tiny Nicoise olives with the very special
taste) followed by stuffed tomatoes and green peppers. In the winter,
he converts to a Lyonnaise lunchroom serving *un machon.* Alex is an
expert on Beaujolais wines. FF250.

Chez Françoise, Aerogare des Invalides (near *le quai* on l'Esplanade des Invalides); tel. 47.05.49.03. Closed Sunday night and Monday. A serious and authentic French restaurant. FF250.

Chez Maître Paul, 12 rue Monsieur-le-Prince, 7th; tel. 43.54.
74.59. Closed Sunday and Monday. A small interesting restaurant
with specialties from the Jura: *les escargots au vin d'Arbois* (snails in
a Jura wine sauce), and *le coq au vin jaune* (fricasseed chicken in white
wine and cream sauce). The place was originally owned by a Monsieur
Paul Maître, who switched his name around to name his restaurant.
It's now in the capable hands of Monsieur Gaugain. Interesting Jura
wines. FF200.

Pasta et Vino, 59 rue Dauphine, 6th; no need to phone.
Crowded, not very comfortable, but no doubt the best pasta in Paris—
and, unfortunately, the worst wine.

Le Petit Nicois, 10 rue Amelie; tel. 25.51.83.65. Closed Sunday and Monday for lunch. A little restaurant with fish specialties. On
Wednesday and Saturday, the restaurant serves a reasonably good
paella. A nice rosé from the Provence.

Le Petit Zinc, 25 rue de Buci, 6th; tel. 43.54.79.34. Open
every day of the week and the year. Once a charming neighborhood restaurant, now a charming part of a mini-chain (including *un brasserie* at
27 rue de Buci, a caterer at 29 rue de Buci, and l'Echaudé at 21 rue de
l'Echaudé). Excellent fresh oysters and seafood. Good, well-cooked
food at a reasonable price. FF200.

Récamier, 4 rue Récamier, 7th; tel. 45.48.86.58. Closed Sunday. This charming place, situated in a little *impasse,* has a sprawling
terrace. One of the specialties is *boeuf bourguignon,* a hearty beef
stew. Pike mousse *(brochet)* with a sauce Nantua and veal kidneys in a
Santenay sauce are also highly recommended. The proprietors recommend the Bourgognes, but there are some excellent Côtes de Rhone as
well. Highly rated in the guidebooks. About FF400.

Chez René, 14 blvd. Saint-Germain, 5th; tel. 43.54.30.23.
Closed Saturday, Sunday, and August. Good hearty Burgundian food
without flourishes. Excellent beaujolais. FF200.

Le Petit Saint-Benoît, 4 rue Saint-Benoît. Closed Saturday
and Sunday. No reservation needed. This has been a student eating
place for so many years the students are all in their 60s. Not as good
as it used to be, but comparatively it is still cheap. Less than FF100.

Le Petit Prince, 12 rue de Lanneau; tel. 43.54.77.26. Open
daily for dinner only; serves until 12:30 a.m. Decorated with bric-a-
brac, it has a flea market atmosphere. A young crowd, late eaters.
Very simple but nice food: *salad aux lardons, terrine de canard,* chicken
legs in *aioli, saumon au beurre nantais, pot-au-feu.* About FF100.

D.P.R. Sud-ouest, 46 ave. de la Bourdonnais; tel. 45.55.
59.59. Open every day until 10 p.m. Behind a boutique where all sorts
of products from the southwest of France are sold there is a restaurant.

The decor is rustic, with hunting trophies and stone walls. You'll be served large portions of a genuine regional cuisine, including *canard* and *foie gras*. Wine by the glass (FF7 to FF18). FF100 or a bit more for a meal.

Bistrot 6, 6 rue des Fosses-Saint-Marcel; tel. 47.07.91.25. Closed Saturday and Sunday. A real *bistrot*, clean and simple with white tablecloths. Good food at honest prices. *Les menus* for FF62 and FF129.

Le Babylone, 13 rue de Babylone, 7th. Closed Sunday; lunches only. One of the very best buys in town. *La cuisine bourgeoise: petit salé, roti de porc, blanquette, boeuf bourguignon, boeuf mode, boeuf gros sel*, etc. Each of those costs only FF14. A complete meal costs about FF50.

Cinnamon, 30 rue Saint-Sulpice, 6th; tel. 43.26.53.33. Closed Sunday. A pleasant atmosphere with photographs of movie stars. Traditional food, including *navarin de ris de veau* (FF70) and *gigot de lotte* (FF68). A full meal for about FF100.

Brasserie Fernand, 13 rue Guisarde, 6th; tel. 43.54.61.47. A hangout for film people with a good atmosphere. *Un brasserie* in front, a restaurant in back. Good food, fair prices. About FF120.

Saints-Pères, 175 blvd. Saint-Germain, 5th; tel. 45.48.56.85. Closed Wednesday. Serves only until 9:30 p.m. Authentic 19th-century atmosphere, including gas lights. This restaurant has been in the same family for three generations. All the traditional French dishes. Less than FF100.

Chez Wajda, 10 rue de la Grande-Chaumière; tel. 43.25.66.90. Closed Saturday and Sunday. Quiet and simple. The food is prepared by Marie and served by her brothers, Leon and Casimir. The place seems a bit faded and, until the food arrives, might be depressing. This is the way one ate regularly in Paris before pizzerias, fast-food, and pinball machines. A neighborhood restaurant that caters to Parisians who love French food. FF50 (can you believe it?).

Aux Trois Canettes—Chez Alexandre, 18 rue des Canettes; tel. 43.26.29.62. This amusing and busy restaurant started as an Italian eatery. Today the chef is Spanish, and his influence is evident despite the still very Italian *carte*. A favorite of the publishers in the neighborhood for lunch. It was favored by such artists as Max Ernst, Man Ray, Calder, Giacometti, and his brother Diego. The food is good if not traditionally Italian or French. About FF100 for dinner, less for lunch or *le menu*.

The 8th and 9th *Arrondissements*

The 8th *arrondissement*, known as les Beaux Quartiers because of the chic and expensive shops, the houses of *haute couture*, the international art galleries, and le faubourg Saint-Honoré, is losing its charm as les Champs-Elysées deteriorates.

More than 200 feet wide with four rows of trees, **les Champs-Elysées** once was the pride of the city of light. But during the last three or four decades it has been neglected somewhat by those who fight to preserve the unique flavor of Paris.

Faceless, flat-windowed walls have replaced the fine old buildings and their quiet dignity. Les Champs-Elysées has become cheap, noisy, and garish. It might have been worse—at one point the beautiful mansions that form **le Rond Point** were scheduled for demolition. The Round Point was saved, but it was too late for the rest of les Champs-Elysées: the theaters, junk-food dispensaries, shopping arcades, and drugstores have changed the character of the street. The great *cafés* have been chopped up; l'Hôtel Claridge has been converted to apartments, banks, airlines, pizzerias, and theaters. Finally, the last holdout was remodeled—the beautiful acre of wicker chairs and little round tables at Fouquet's is now an enclosed glass terrace, like any *café* anywhere in the city.

Today, tourists in shorts and sandals, some shirtless, crowd the sidewalks. Who knows why they are here. (Perhaps looking for the city's *Bureau de Tourisme* at number 121?) The once beautiful boulevard has become a boardwalk.

Or most of it has. From le Rond Point to la place de la Concorde, les Champs-Elysées remains untouched. It is still one of the great strolls in this changing world. **Le Petit Palais** and **le Grand Palais** are excellent museums with choice exhibits changing several times a year. Le Petit Palais itself is a show. It's worth the effort simply to go in and walk in the marbled courtyard with its statuary and fountain. One can sit here on a clear, cold day, out of the wind, basking in the winter sun, and absorbing the splendor and elegance of another age.

Starting at the Church of Saint-Philippe-de-Roule, walk **le faubourg-Saint-Honoré** all the way to la rue Castiglione. Besides the world's most elegant shops, you will pass **le Palais Elysée** (France's White House), the elegant **Hôtel Bristol**, the **American ambassador's residence** at number 39, the **British Embassy** at number 35, **la rue Royale** (with a view of the Madeleine church to the left), **la place de la Concorde,** and **le Palais Bourbon** to the right. At la rue Castiglione, turn left and go through la place Vendôme to la rue de la Paix. You have seen the most elegant and expensive things Paris has to offer.

For some reason many Americans go wild over the food and wine emporium called **Fauchon.** It is a collection of exotic (and sometimes not so exotic, including Salinas lettuce and Campbell's soup) food from all over the world. Such shops must exist in large American cities. Why not instead explore things that are not found in America? The little *charcuteries* (butchers specializing in pork), the butchers specializing in game, the cremeries selling farm-fresh unpasteurized cheese, *les boulangeries* filled with the beautiful smell of freshly baked bread, *pâtisseries* of every kind, and fishmongers with unheard-of specimens, all fresh, glistening, and smelling of the sea.

The broad, elegant, and quiet **tree-lined boulevards** such as l'avenue Hoche are also pleasant to walk. At the end of l'avenue Hoche there is an entrance to le Parc Monceau, which, in the 18th century, was the private park of the duke of Orléans.

The 9th *Arrondissement*

The southern border of the 9th *arrondissement* follows the site of the wall that ran along the north perimeter of Paris prior to 1670. When this barrier was torn down and the town expanded, it left a four-mile-long ribbon of devastation from the future site of le Madeleine to the Bastille. This space was eventually converted to a wide, tree-lined promenade. The word *boulevard* comes from the defensive rampart or "bulwark" it replaced.

Les grands boulevards are really one continuous promenade. It is referred to in the plural because it has different names at different parts of its length: *les boulevards* Saint-Martin, Saint-Denis, Bonne Nouvelle, Poissonnière, Montmartre, and des Italians; then, after l'Opéra, Capucines and Madeleine.

Created at the end of the 17th century, *les grands boulevards* remained virtually deserted for nearly 100 years. But eventually the wonderful open space in what had become the center of town attracted the rich, who built sumptuous town houses along the edges. Thus decorated, *les boulevards* became a favorite strolling place for Parisians, who, for the most part, lived on narrow, crowded streets.

In time, these strollers attracted *les marchands de limonade,* who dispensed drinks to thirsty pedestrians from pushcarts. These, in turn, led to *cafés* that filled the wide sidewalks with tables and chairs providing passers-by a place to rest as well as to be refreshed.

In due course, theaters, music halls, cabarets, restaurants, and other places of commercial entertainment filled the area. People gathered on *les boulevards* to gossip, to see and to be seen, and to exchange artistic and literary ideas or opinions. All classes of society rubbed shoulders on *les boulevards*: officers, lawyers, gentlemen, priests, financiers, foreigners, fine ladies, demi-mondaines. The noun *boule-vardier* was coined to describe the habitués, who represented the art of living well.

By the end of the 19th century, *les boulevards* had become the hub of Parisian life. *Le boulevardier* was traditionally a special person, usually of some note and always with a special talent for coming up with *un mot juste*.

Many *cafés* along *les boulevards* became famous. Each had fiercely loyal clients who regarded "their" *café* more or less as their private club. "A man will change his religion sooner than change his *café*," one wit of the day remarked.

Strolling is now, unfortunately, a lost art. The busy *boulevards* are still tree-lined and wide, but as in many parts of Paris, the automobile rules. *Le boulevardier* has become a frantic driver and his *mot juste* is the blast of an ear-piercing *klaxon* (horn).

Since 1882 **le Musée Grévin,** on le boulevard Montmartre, has given Parisians waxwork glimpses of the past. The famous and infamous characters of French history—François I, Louis XIV, Charlotte Corday, Marie-Antoinette, the Revolutionary tribunals, Napoleon—are all here. Le Musée Grévin is as much a part of the Paris scene as Madame Toussaud's is a part of London. There are a great many theaters in the area, and for anyone interested in stage design and costume, **le Musée de l'Opéra et Bibliothèque** is a must. It exhibits models of stage sets, costumes, and other mementos of famous operas and stars.

La Nouvelle Athènes, a small wedge between la rue Notre-Dame-de-Lorette and la rue des Martyrs, has some remarkable architectural sights. It is so called because of the frequent use of columns and the neoclassic style inspired by ancient Greek architecture. Most of these buildings, built during the French Restoration, contribute to a calm and pleasant atmosphere. It's a good neighborhood in which to stroll. And the idea of doing so is not new. During the 19th century, the area became popular with street strollers known as *les lorettes*. As Balzac tried to describe her: "*Une lorette* is a proper word used to describe the position of a young girl in an activity difficult to, in modesty, refer to, as l'Académie Française neglected to define it, which is understandable in view of the age of its 40 members."

Close by at 80 rue Taitbout, just outside the triangle, you will find **la place d'Orléans.** Its Doric porticos and callandes and a pleasant fountain create the air of an Italian palazzo. This square, which has been completely restored, was acquired in 1822 by Mademoiselle Mar, a leading lady of 19th-century French theater. It became very chic when Georges Sand and Chopin (there are plaques on the house fronts) took houses here. They brought their friends, including the sculptor Dantan, Alexandre Dumas, *père*, and other notables of the period.

Have a look at **la rue d'Aumale,** inaugurated during the reign of Louis-Philippe. The beautiful facades are typical of the period. Then go to **la place Saint-Georges** for a look at number 28, a curious house in a "romantic-troubadour" style. At number 2 is a house that was burned down during the Commune and identically rebuilt almost a century later in 1872.

There is much more to see in this section, easily found by simply ambling around. **Le Musée Renan Scheffer,** installed in a beautiful mansion at 16 rue Chaptal, has a collection of mementos of the novelist and feminist Georges Sand and her epoch. It is open 10 a.m. to 5:40 p.m. except Monday.

Recommended Restaurants

There are many restaurants in these quarters, but these few deserve extra mention:

Chez André, 12 rue Marbeuf, 8th; tel. 47.20.59.57. Closed Tuesday. Not *une brasserie* but a bit like one in character and bill of fare. It has served excellent dishes for more than 35 years. Don't worry about waiting for a table, everyone does. It's worth it. FF200.

L'Artois, 13 rue d'Artois, 8th; tel. 42.25.01.10. Closed Sunday and July 14 to the beginning of September. The fare here is principally Auvergnat: ham, Correze blood sausage *(boudin)*, etc. A bit heavy but not difficult to digest. Some wines from the Massif Central not often found in Paris. Nice atmosphere. FF250.

Fouquet's, 99 ave. des Champs-Elysées, 8th; tel. 47.23.70.60. The upstairs is closed Saturday and Sunday. The restaurant is upstairs, but the grill on the ground floor is also good, and it never closes. Expensive upstairs (FF400). The cost downstairs depends on what you eat. Some dishes are a bargain.

Marius et Janetten, 4 ave. George V, 8th; tel. 47.23.41.88. Closed Saturday, Sunday, and August. In the summer the terrace is as delightful as the splendid fish dishes served here. Expensive. FF450.

Val d'Isère, 2 rue de Berri, 8th; tel. 43.59.12.66. Closed August. A good place to eat in les Champs-Elysées area at any time. As one might guess, the food tends to be Alpine but offers a large choice. About FF200 for a full meal.

L'Alsace, 39 ave. des Champs-Elysées, 8th; tel. 43.59.44.24. Open every day, all night, year-round. Good oysters and seafood all year. Sauerkraut *(choucroute)* and other Alsatian specialties. About FF200.

The 10th, 11th, and 12th *Arrondissements*

Many visitors pass through a part of the 10th *arrondissement* when leaving one of the major train stations, la Gare du Nord or la Gare de l'Est. But that is often the limit of contact with this part of town. Apart from the two stations, the only other points of possible interest are two large hospitals and le Canal Saint-Martin, which runs through the 10th from north to south.

But changes are afoot. Ten years ago, a plan to revise and improve the eastern part of Paris was adopted by the city council. A massive project, it includes most of the 10th, 11th, 12th, 13th, 18th, and 20th *arrondissements*. This covers a vast area of nearly 10,000 acres, or 45% of Paris (excluding *le bois*), with a population in the neighborhood of one million. The plan calls for physical changes in the character of the area that are intended to attract a population with a higher income.

The plans include 23,000 new living units, 33 acres of park along the banks of the Seine, 6 miles of walking paths, a tree-lined pedestrian area between the Bastille and le bois de Vincennes, 94 acres of gardens, the construction of 2 new bridges across the Seine, 37 acres of new roads, and 11 acres of playing fields. Light industry and artisan activity will be encouraged.

Le Canal Saint-Martin

A total of 80 miles of canals, with 1,480 acres of verdant canal banks, pass through the Paris area. The longest is **le Canal de l'Ourcy**. It runs for the most part outside Paris, but in town it runs through the 19th from le Bassin de la Villette and out of town. The longest canal inside Paris is **le Canal Saint-Martin**. It runs from the Seine through the Arsenal basin, goes underground through the 11th *arrondissement*, and then surfaces in the 10th. It connects the Ourcy canal to the Seine.

In the 19th century, canals provided an inexpensive and dependable means of transporting merchandise and other goods within the interior of France and between Paris and the rest of France. They brought firewood in from the forest of Retz, cereals from Brie, wine from Burgundy, and imports from and exports to *le havre* (the harbor). Paris' place in history is in part due to its situation on a long navigable river. The oldest seal of the city of Paris is emblazoned with a ship, indicating the importance of the city as a port. Paris is still the first river port and the fourth most important port overall of France.

In 1802, it was decided to connect Paris with the country's canal complex. The Villette basin, 2,400 feet long and 24 feet wide, was

36

begun in 1806 and finished in 1809. It serves to feed the
Paris and to provide water for cleaning the city streets.
though the canals are still used commercially, pleasure boat.
Paris and other French canals far outnumber those carrying freig.
A project to turn the canal into an autoroute during the 1960s was
abandoned. Le Canal Saint-Martin today is a "green lane." Along its
banks and on the embankments of the Villette basin, an urban reno-
vation project is under way. The old rundown buildings, the warehouses, and the abandoned factories are being converted into
residences, artists' studios, lofts, and modern industrial plants.

Four years ago, a pleasure boat marina was developed in the section of le Canal Saint-Martin known as **l'Arsenal** (the spot was at
one time the city's defense arsenal). Today a pleasant landscaped
marina (directly south of the Bastille on the edge of the 12th),
l'Arsenal accommodates 185 boats. There is also a visitor's dock for 5
to 10 boats. The basin is 1,785 feet long and 130 to 230 feet wide. It
can accommodate boats with a 4 1/3-foot draft, and the entrance lock
(from the Seine) can handle boats up to 17 feet above water level. A
restaurant that serves as a tea room between meals has opened on the
quay side. For particulars write Captainerie du Port du Arsenal,
boulevard de la Bastille, 75011, Paris.

Two excursion boats make regular trips along the Paris water-
ways: Canauxrame (tel. 46.24.86.16) and Quizz Tour Paris Canal (tel.
48.74.75.30). Up to half-day scheduled cruises operate all summer.

Elsewhere in the 11th and 12th

The 11th and 12th *arrondissements* both developed outside the city
walls established by Charles V. Here artisans, especially furniture
makers, live and have their studios. The eastern end of the 11th, once
part of the village of Charonne, also has many cul-de-sacs with artists'
studios and workshops.

For many years, the 11th and 12th were dominated by Auvergnats
and Bretons, but today these *arrondissements* have become more cosmopolitan. Later arrivals include Arabs, North Africans, Israelis,
Moroccans, Turks, West Indians, Vietnamese, and Thais. Each ethnic
group clusters around their own grocery stores and restaurants.

There is a plan afoot to convert an unused railroad viaduct that
runs from the Bastille to Vincennes into a tree-lined walkway. The viaduct, 20 to 25 feet high, consists of a series of large brick arches
occupied by little bars, restaurants, shops, warehouses, and artisan's
workshops. These will remain, and more bars and restaurants will be
added along the walkway above. If this actually comes about, it will

37

create a pleasant verdant walk in a part of town virtually unknown to the average visitor.

An old-fashioned flea market in la place d'Aligre, situated next to a covered food market, is one of the few junk and old clothes *marchés* that has not converted to antiques. It is between la rue du faubourg Saint-Antoine and l'avenue Daumesnil in the 12th.

The smallest house in Paris is located at 39 rue de Château-d'Eau. It is no more than a ground floor plus one story measuring 15 feet high and a bit more than 3 feet wide.

Recommended Restaurants

There are not many recommended restaurants in this part of town, but the ones below are traditional and good. (*Michelin* lists a total of 23 for all three *arrondissements; Gault and Millau* are a bit more generous.)

Astier, 44 rue Jean-Pierre-Timbaud, 11th; tel. 43.57.16.35. Closed Saturday and Sunday. This is what is known as *un bistrot du quartier,* meaning that it caters to people in the immediate neighborhood. Since it appeared in the *Gault and Millau* guide, however, it is no longer local. But you'll eat well and for less than FF100.

Brasserie Flo, 7 Cours des Petites Ecuries, 10th; tel. 47.70. 13.59. Open every day; closed August; serves until 1:30 a.m. One of the best known *brasseries* in all Paris, and one of the best. Le Flo is in a court off 73 rue du faubourg Saint-Denis. Excellent shellfish and oysters. It was opened in 1885, and the decor matches the era. Now owned by an Alsatian who has a half-dozen *brasseries* around town (all good). Less than FF200 a person.

Julien, 16 faubourg Saint-Denis, 10th; tel. 47.70.12.06. Open every day; closed July. One of le Flo group of *brasseries*, also with authentic late 19th-century decor. Excellent *brasserie* fare, but no shellfish or oysters. One can eat well here for less than FF200.

Sousceyrac, 35 rue Faidherbe, 11th; tel. 43.71.65.30. This family restaurant has been rated with one star by *Michelin* for at least three decades. Specialties from Gascony. The pâté and *les terrines* are exceptional, as is *le cassoulet*. More than FF200 a person.

Train Bleu, in la Gare de Lyon; tel. 43.43.09.06. Before leaving by train for la Côte d'Azur, Africa, or the Near East in the old days, this was where you dined. A splendidly restored *Belle Epoque* decor. Good food, but a bit expensive. FF230.

Chez Nick, 13 rue Taylor, 10th; tel. 42.08.89.72. There are probably a dozen or more places like Nick's in these *arrondissements*. This is the only one we've found so far, however. No decoration at all,

38

but excellent Marseillaise food. FF140.

Terminus Nord, 23 rue de Dunkerque, 10th; tel. 42.85. 05.15. Decorated in 1925 style, this is also perfect for a meal before taking the train to London. Good *brasserie* food, very professionally served by waiters in black vests and white aprons.

The 13th, 14th, and 15th *Arrondissements*

Perhaps one of the least-known neighborhoods to Parisians themselves, the 13th *arrondissement* has also suffered the most under the "modernization of Paris" program.

The very first of the concrete high-rise eyesores that have all but destroyed the Paris horizon was built here in 1958. Today, a half-dozen modern complexes have taken the place of modest, two-story workingmen's homes.

In the 15th century, the little river Bièvre wound its way to the Seine outside the Paris city walls. (The Bièvre gets its name from its earliest user, the beaver. The Celtic word for beaver is *befar*.) Later, houses with second-story balconies and ground-floor tanneries crowded its banks. Animal hides, in the curing process, were washed in the water of the stream. In spite of the resulting pollution, the crowded riverside maintained a picturesque rustic charm. Possibly it was these qualities that attracted Flemish dyers who set up factories along the stream. The beer-drinking Belgians added pleasure gardens and open-air

The Bièvre, a river in the 13th arrondissement.

bals (balls) to the riverside activities.

More and more establishments grew on the banks. In 1860, from the Paris city limits to where the Bièvre emptied into the Seine, there were 9 laundries, a paper mill, a wood washing depot, 2 distilleries, a blanket laundry, a powder factory, 3 dye manufacturers, a glue factory, a depot for fresh skins from the stockyards, 24 tanneries, 2 flour mills, 21 leather tawers, 7 leatherworkers, 3 *brasseries*, 2 cotton-thread manufacturers, 1 wool-thread manufacturer, 4 dyers, 2 cardboard factories, 4 old clothes laundries, 8 laundry wash houses, 2 skin dressers, 1 color-grinding factory, 1 soap factory, 1 wool laundry, and 1 acid, soap, and candle factory. The Bièvre brought prosperity to the Left Bank.

The water, used for so many purposes, emitted a strong and unpleasant odor. A study was made between 1840 and 1848 for cleaning the Bièvre, and although some progress was made, no plan was effective. Finally, the river was covered and used as a sewer. It is no longer visible anywhere along its course inside Paris.

Among the Flemish dyers was a family called Gobelins that quickly gained wealth and fame with the extraordinary colors they created in their fabric dyes. They brought their art to such a degree of perfection that Colbert, Louis XIV's finance minister, bought the whole operation and turned it into a royal factory. As the Gobelins' factory grew, 250 workmen, each with his own house and garden, created a thriving community in the area. It was the beginning of what is today the 13th *arrondissement*.

During the same period when the Gobelins' enterprise was bought by the crown, l'Hôpital General was created to help the sick people of Paris. It was built on the site of an arsenal that used saltpeter in the manufacture of powder, and became known as *la salpêtrière*. At its center is a

The banks of the Bièvre in the Gobelins gardens.

church in the shape of a Greek cross. The four chapels, divided into eight areas, served to separate patients with communicable diseases. Throughout the century, this hospital has been used as a home for

40

paupers, prostitutes, and the insane, especially insane women. This hospital, too, was located in the confines of what became the 13th *arrondissement*.

Balloons Above the 13th

The 13th saw history made on a September day in 1783. On le Butte-Aux-Cailles, a desolate hillside inhabited by a few creaking windmills, Pilatre de Rozier and the Marquis d'Arlandes landed their hot air balloon after a 25-minute flight of about five miles. It was the first balloon to carry a man and float free.

Otherwise this *arrondissement* gained little notoriety as it grew into a workingman's quarter with factories, several hospitals, a prison, tanneries, and, of course, the Gobelins' tapestry industry. Evidence of the financial status of the residents is noted when, in the latter part of the 19th century, the first horse-meat butcher in Paris appeared at la place d'Italie. Victor Hugo also found it appropriate to set several scenes from *les Misérables* here.

Today, a half-dozen modern tower complexes, most of an exceptionally mundane design, cast their shadows on the few remaining old neighborhoods. If not beautiful, however, the 13th is still interesting.

A Tour Through the 13th

From le boulevard de l'Hôpital (metro Saint-Marcel; bus 91 or 57) find an entrance in the wall that surrounds l'Hôpital Salpêtrière. Once inside the wall follow the signs to the Chapel of Saint-Louis. This is really worth seeing and just about the only tourist site in this section of town. It is covered in detail in the *Michelin Green Guide*. The eight formerly separate areas are evident, though no longer divided. Only two are still used as chapels, the rest—at the moment— house a scattering of bigger-than-life wooden sculptures marring the beautiful symmetry of space and decorated stone. The history of the hospital is interesting enough to warrant a good and careful look. The little parks and streets within the walls are beautifully planted.

The neighborhood just behind le Salpêtrière has become an architect's nightmare. Before train tracks from la Gare d'Austerlitz penetrated it, the area was a village (Ivry) of modest two-story houses, low storage sheds, ateliers, and horse barns. Most of the dwellings had neat gardens or back yards. It is now a hodgepodge of new, quasi-modern, redecorated, and false-fronted houses that never cease to amaze but seldom charm. The entire neighborhood has an air of self-destruction, but it's worth exploring if you really want to know Paris.

To see the rest of the Ivry neighborhood, walk down la rue du

Chevaleret, cutting over to la rue Dunois on one street and back on the other. It is easy to see the old pattern of two-story houses with gardens and the new pattern of higher, colorful, and almost freakish designs.

On la rue Charcot is a bright yellow and orange paneled building accommodating an oriental meditation center. At 119 rue du Chevaleret, behind an unmarked door, is a convent of Polish nuns. From the streets on either side one can see a simple belfry on the roof, and there appears to be a garden hidden by high walls. Next to the convent is an Irish *café* smelling more like stale beer than the old sod. The next door leads to a long, decrepit courtyard not noteworthy except for two red towers in the very rear that don't seem to belong to the house they're attached to.

Around the corner at 14-16 rue Domremy is a new (or completely remodeled) building that is difficult to describe. It seems to be built behind a wall with windows (the facade of the house originally on the spot?), and there is an extraordinary green-lawned backyard with a descending cement stairway and what appear to be two doghouses. The doghouses are ventilators, and the stairway leads to an underground garage.

At 1 rue Dunois there is a restaurant with an uncommon bill of fare that includes wild boar and mountain goat. Even more bizarre is its name, *Au Pet Lapin,* which translates to "At the Rabbit's Fart."

Farther down la rue du Chevaleret is the first modern building in the 13th, the **Salvation Army headquarters,** designed by le Corbusier.

All of the 13th is under reconstruction. There are no more high-rises but many small units of 8 to 10 apartments, some with interesting features, such as outside stairways, connecting bridges, open courts, and high-arched passageways between streets and courts. Although this back-water neighborhood does not say "Paris," it has a certain charm that is unusual enough to claim a tourist's interest. The neighborhood is very self-sufficient, with its own markets and shops, theaters, movie houses, and cultural activities. Those who live here do not leave often; when they do go to other parts of Paris, even for a short visit, they say "I'm going to Paris."

The southern side of the 13th is less bedraggled, but more drastically changed. Very tall apartment houses and towers (20 to 30 stories and higher) have transformed the once bucolic banks of the Bièvre into a Manhattanized Chinatown. Still, there are a few traces of the old 13th to be found. At 65 blvd. Arago, *la Cité Fleurie,* a group of artists' studios in a delightful garden, has withstood drooling real estate developers since the 1880s. The two-story studio/apartments are on a bluff with southern exposure. They have known notable occupants: Gauguin, Modigliani, Rodin, Bourdelle, Maillot. The gate is unlocked, and you can have a nice stroll through this island of gardens, many crowded with the sculpture of the resident artists. There is a path in back leading through *la Cité Verte* down the steep hill to the street below.

Walk the streets around la place de Rungis, la rue Bourgon, le Moulin de Prés. There are a few small but elegant single-family houses among the many larger units under construction.

The 14th *Arrondissement*: An Artist's Haven

The 14th *arrondissement* has also taken a severe beating in recent decades. It must have been scheduled for complete renewal by the Pompidou planners. They began in 1961 and completed la Tour Montparnasse (the highest in Europe) in 1973. But the "renewing" goes on.

The Mount of Parnassas—the classical seat of poetry and music—was the name given to the quarter by students who came here during the 17th century when Queen Margot appropriated university land along the Seine.

During the 19th century, Montparnasse was pleasantly rural and close enough to the city center to be reached on foot from most parts of Paris. It became a favorite summer picnic and meeting place. Eventually, clever promoters opened dance pavilions and restaurants that became known as *les guinguettes* (pleasure gardens, probably from *guindal,* the 18th-century slang for group drinking). Many of *les guinguettes* were little more than pavilions with straw roofs, and most eventually disappeared in fires. **La Closerie des Lilas** (the Lilac Garden) is the sole survivor from that period. It is now a bar and restaurant with a delightful summer terrace. The food is good but expensive, and the bar is pleasantly decorated but wretchedly operated (I once waited more than an hour for service). The rich, pretentious clients add little to the atmosphere.

Between the World Wars, the 14th enjoyed the reputation of being the "new artists' quarter." Most of the painters of the Paris School of the 1920s and 1930s left Montmartre for Montparnasse. They settled into the little dead-end streets and mews where horse barns were converted to studios. Traces of this period are still found throughout the quarter. At 83 rue de la Tombe d'Issoire is a good example—la Cité Annibal. On the next block off la rue des Artistes is la Villa Ganguet. Also notable, albeit from a later period, are la Villa Jarnet at 105 rue Didot, la Villa Leone at la rue Bardinet, l'Impasse Florimont at 150 rue Alesia, and la Villa Seurat at 101 de la Tombe Issoire (Henry

Miller wrote *Tropic of Cancer* here, and Anais Nin lived in one of the studios with Lawrence Durrell).

Montparnasse has been well known to Americans since the 1920s when the *cafés* on both sides of the broad boulevard Montparnasse were favorites of expatriate writers and artists. The Russian refugees were the first to discover Montparnasse, and there is still an excellent Russian restaurant called Dominique on la rue Vavin near le boulevard Raspail. The expatriate Americans described in post-World War I American writing congregated in the *cafés* that still exist in this neighborhood. **La Coupole**, the most popular today, attracts an "in" crowd that enjoys watching and being watched. **Le Café Select** across the street has remained almost exactly as it was 60 years ago; there is always at least one chess game in progress inside. On the same side of *le boulevard* is a vestige of **la Rotonde,** now mostly devoted to being a movie house. Le Select was the most popular *café* in the salad days of the quarter, at least until a dispute during which Malcolm Cowley and the French novelist Louis Aragon took a poke at the owner. Then everyone moved to the shady side of the street—to le Dome and la Coupole.

Le Parc Montsouris, the second largest park in Paris, is a delicious breathing space. It has a large artificial lake, pleasant walking paths, large open lawns, and many old, rare, and interesting trees. On a bluff in the park is the replica of the palace of the Beys in Tunis, moved here from its place at the International Exposition of 1867. It is almost in ruins, and every year it is scheduled to be restored.

On the rim of the 14th and at the edge of town, near le Parc Montsouris, you will find **la Cité Universitaire**, living quarters for foreign students in Paris. This too is a pleasant place for a quiet walk and a breath of fresh air. It is reminiscent of a New England college campus, but with a broad range of interesting architecture drawn from the participating countries.

For anyone still interested in Vladimir Ilich Ulyanov, later known as Lenin, the houses he lived in when he was in Paris from 1908 to 1912 are at 24 rue Beaunier and a few blocks away at 4 rue Marie Rose (25 rue Sarrette). At 4 rue Marie Rose there is a plaque on the wall and a little museum (visits by appointment; tel. 43.22.82.38). Lenin spent a lot of time in a *café* at 11 ave. General-Leclerc (then l'avenue d'Orléans). He also spent a lot of time in le Parc Montsouris, which he called "my private garden."

Behind la Gare Montparnasse, along the railroad tracks, a large part of the neighborhood is known as Plaisance, or Pleasure. (The name was given to the area when an enterprising real estate dealer was trying to attract customers—unfortunately the quarter never was able to live

44

up to the name.) Most of la Plaisance was recently torn down to erect low-cost housing and some offices. The new buildings have done little to improve the neighborhood. But one, designed by the Spanish architect Ricardo Bofill, is definitely worth a look.

Critics have described Bofill's work with such epithets as "papier-mâché architecture," "lamentable parody," "neo-fascist hustling," "Stalinist Atlantic wall." His colleagues are unanimous in their abuse of his work. Every one of his projects raises passionate denunciation. The one in la Plaisance is in a housing unit referred to as "Guilleminot-Vercingetorix" after the streets it borders. It must be seen to be hated or loved. The buildings consist of two circles backed by a large half circle, creating two closed courts and one large open one. The construction is unprecedented, with columned glass walls and unusual and surprising turns and shapes everywhere. One side is being reserved for low-cost housing, the other for "middle rents," and whatever remains for office space.

At 59 rue Vercingetorix stands one of the few old structures left in the area: a modest workingman's chapel appropriately called l'Eglise Notre-Dame-du-Travail-de-Plaisance (Church of Our Lady of Work at Plaisance). Built in 1899-1901, it has steel construction beams under the roof rather than the usual wooden ones. This creates the fitting atmosphere of the interior of a factory. The beams were salvaged from le Palais de l'Industrie exhibit at the International Exposition of 1900. The bell in the tower, removed from a smaller demolished church around the corner, also has a history. A gift from Napoleon III in 1865, it was loot from Sebastopol after the battle of Crimea.

La rue Daguerre (near Denfert-Rochereau) is a pleasant walking/food/shopping street, animated on weekends when the food vendors shout for your attention. There is an unusual fish shop that can only be described as a fish *charcuterie*, or delicatessen, with many mouthwatering morsels for sale.

The 15th *Arrondisement*: Artists Amid the "Cement Age"

The 15th is the largest and most densely populated *arrondissement* of Paris, with more than 200,000 inhabitants. It extends from the Seine to la Gare Montparnasse.

In le Passage de Dantzig (at 52 rue Dantzig) there is a curious round structure, a vestige of the Exposition of 1900. Its grilled entrances led to the door of the Palace of Women. It is a round building, each floor with wedge-shaped artist's studios used by many now-famous painters. These cells—there were 80 of them—understandably

45

gave the name *la Ruche* (Beehive) to the structure. Sculptors were on the ground floor, painters and engravers above.

Until a few years ago, *un abattoir* (slaughterhouse) existed at the corner of la rue Brancion and la rue des Morillons. Recently it was converted into a large public park, named after the late poet, composer, and singer Georges Brassens. It has large playgrounds and lots of benches, making it an excellent place to relax. An unusual feature is the "Garden of Odors," designed so that the blind, too, may enjoy this little bit of nature.

Along the Left Bank of the Seine from le boulevard de Grenelle to l'avenue Emile-Zola is a cluster of high-rise buildings housing super-markets, shopping malls, restaurants, department stores, and hotels. It is a classic example of French "Cement Age" architecture, characteristic of Paris building since World War II. It is a cold, unfriendly affair of solid surfaces, sharp corners, undecorated facades, dark passages, and sunless terraces. Called le Beaugrenelle, it appears to rent readily, and the Japanese hotel in its midst prospers. Nearby, on the mid-river island *Allée des Cygnes* (Swan Walk, but the name comes from a mis-pronunciation of the name of the Seine), stands the newly renovated small-scale copy of the Statue of Liberty, donated to France by the American Colony of Paris in 1885. (There are two other copies of the statue in Paris: in the chapel of le Musée des Arts et Métiers, 3rd, and in le Jardin de Luxembourg, 6th.)

What may be the largest leisure center in Europe is a subject much discussed at Paris city hall these days. Monsieur Chirac has a plan for the construction of an "Aquaboulevard" that will include a 180-meter-long water toboggan, artificial storms, a river, water canyons, artificial beaches with tides, a lagoon of marine animals, scuba diving, water massage, waterfalls, a perfumed stream, and a deep-sea trip. This fantastic aqua complex will double as a sports center. Chirac hopes to open it to the people of Paris in 1989. The complex will be near la Porte de Sèvres and is estimated to cost 200-million francs ($33.3 million).

Recommended Restaurants

There are many very good restaurants in the 14th, a few in the 15th, but aside from the Chinese and other Asiatic restaurants, there is not a great choice in the 13th.

Les Marronniers, 53*bis* blvd. Arago, 14th; tel. 47.07.58.57. Closed Sunday. *Les marronniers* are the huge chestnut trees that you'll see lining *le boulevard*. A nice place to eat outdoors; very good classic French food. About FF250.

Au Petit Marguery, 9 blvd. Port Royal, 13th; tel. 43.31.58. 59. Closed Sunday and Monday. Quite nice, unusual food, prepared and served professionally. Breast of duck with fresh figs and raisins, roast pigeon with wild mushrooms, turbot with lobster and chervil sauce are examples of the fare. Just less than FF300.

L'Assiette, 181 rue du Château, 14th; tel. 43.22.64.86. Closed Monday and Tuesday. Excellent dishes that are not found everywhere, including *pintadeau* (guinea hen) in cabbage, suckling deer, and other seasonal things. FF190.

Le Bar á Huitres, 112 blvd. Montparnasse, 14th; tel. 43.20. 71.01. The only place in Paris where you can order just one oyster. Excellent seafood. Sit at the counter and have a platter of mixed shell-fish. About FF180 for a full meal.

Le Bourbonnais, 29 rue Delambre, 14th; tel. 43.20.61.73. Closed Saturday noon and Sunday. A serious chef, an excellent choice of a variety of dishes all done in an honest classical manner. Figure about FF200.

Chez Grand-Mère, 92 rue Broca, 13th; tel. 74.07.13.65. Open for dinner only; closed Sunday. Down-to-earth dishes, including *le pot-au-feu, la potée* (boiled vegetables with bacon), *la langue de mouton en ragout,* and a very special camembert. About FF120.

Le Dôme, 108 blvd. Montparnasse, 14th; tel. 43.35.25.81. Closed Monday. This was one of the famous Montparnasse sidewalk *cafés.* A few years ago it was redecorated to the teeth in gay nineties style. Today it is a fish restaurant—and a very good one—though no longer a *café.* There is one steak on the bill of fare, everything else comes from the sea. About FF275.

La Popotière, 35 rue du Banquier, 13th; tel. 43.31.40.25. Closed Saturday noon and Sunday. Some interesting specialties, in-cluding breast of duck with raspberry vinegar and red currants, potted duck with mushrooms, *le ris de veau,* and couscous on Friday and Saturday. About FF150.

Le Traiteur, 28 rue de la Glacière, 13th; tel. 43.31.64.17. Closed Saturday and Sunday. Back-of-the-stove cooking with a coun-try flavor. FF200.

The 16th and 17th *Arrondissements*

In 1890 when the villages of Auteuil and Passy, adjacent to Paris, were incorporated into the city, they formed a new *arrondissement.* As Paris at that time had only 12 *arrondissements*, the new one was given the designation of 13th. Parisians, used to thinking of Paris as 12

47

arrondissements, would refer to an unmarried man and woman living together as having been "married in the 13th."

The old 13th is now the 16th and is where the upper crust prefers to live. Some of the fine old tree-lined *boulevards* have newly created scars in the forms of expensive new buildings inflicted by real estate promoters. As in other parts of Paris, the 16th is divided into "villages": Auteuil, Passy, le Trocadéro, l'Etoile, and le Bois de Boulogne.

At the Races

by Brendan Murphy

The focal point of interest in Auteuil is the race track, although it is really in le Bois de Boulogne. One considerable advantage of playing the horses at l'Hippodrome d'Auteuil is that it is the easiest race track to reach in the Paris area. The racing ground's gates stand just outside the exit of la Porte d'Auteuil station on le Boulogne line of the Paris metro. From here, just two francs and a short walk through a pedestrian underpass are all you need to reach *la pelouse,* the grassy infield of the track.

It is worthwhile, however, to pay the additional 18 francs it costs for entry to *la tribune,* or grandstand, and the paddock area behind it. Ernest Hemingway, who subsidized the American novel on his winnings here and at Enghien, once explained why:

"You had to watch a jumping race from the top of the stands at Auteuil," he wrote in *A Moveable Feast,* "and it was a fast climb up to see what each horse did and see the horse that might have won and did not, and see why or maybe how he did not do what he could have done."

When Hemingway spoke of a "jumping race" he meant a steeplechase—what the French call *l'obstacle.* That is the kind of racing that has gone on at Auteuil since its gates opened in 1873.

There are two *pelouses,* whose names reflect 19th-century French pride in colonial possessions: le Madagascar, closest to the entrance, with a large tiered viewing platform; and le Tonkin, farther to the north. You are permitted to cross between them only between races, when the barriers are raised for a few minutes.

Because of the FF2 admission, *la pelouse* is the domain of the common man. The class system is still more or less in effect at Auteuil, in the same half-hearted way that first-class carriages still run in the metro. There is a fairly clear disparity between *les pelousards* and those in the stands. *Les pelousards,* largely the working class or immigrants, queue up at the FF10 windows, while their more *bour-*

geois cousins in the stands can afford to risk a FF50 bet or two.

But life on *la pelouse* has advantages other than economy. Here, one is at horse level, and if betting is not a prime consideration it is nice to stroll out by the backstretch to watch as a crowd of horses and riders fly past with the muffled staccato thud of hooves on grass, then sail over the next hedge, fence, or ditch. Unseated riders lend an added thrill to the proceedings.

There is something particularly inspiring about the races here on a Saturday or Sunday in the autumn when the trees have turned but the grass is still summer green and the needle of la Tour Eiffel in the irrelevant city yonder threads a pure blue sky. And there is something elementary and fine in the stately progress of the jockeys in their gaudy colors, diminishing almost from sight as they move up the far stretch along l'Allée des Fortifications toward the turn on the upper end of le Tonkin.

For all its tradition, Auteuil has a modern computerized betting system. This doesn't prevent long lines from developing, however. The answer is to arm oneself with many FF10 coins and feed the automatic betting machines. For those who understand track numbers, there is a computer in the clubhouse under the stands. It can be seen through a glass window as it spits out odds, results, payoffs, and so on, both for this track and the national off-track establishments.

Le Pari Mutuel Urbain, or PMU, is the state off-track betting office. It has branches in thousands of *cafés* across the country. The most popular bet by far is *le tierce,* a trifecta to Americans. This nationally subscribed race is usually the third or fourth on the card either at Auteuil or Longchamp, or at Deauville during August.

La tierce is followed with great interest because something like eight-million Frenchmen are betting on it, and whoever picks the first three horses in the right order stands to win several hundred thousand dollars. *La tierce* bets cannot be placed at the track, which is why neighborhood *cafés* of Paris are so crowded on Sunday mornings.

The routine is to order a cup of coffee or *un pastis* and study *Paris-Turf* and the dailies to see what horses the so-called experts favor. Combinations must be numbered in ink on pre-printed forms, then the edge of the folded form is nipped above the columns where a horse has been indicated. (Check the fold to see that the carbon system works.)

Le tabac counter sells little implements used to snip the edges of the forms. Called *les pinces,* they cost just two francs. Bets can be placed in several amounts, but the most common is the one using the red, or 5-franc, form, which allows for multiple *tierce* combinations at a reasonable investment.

Of course, the odds of scoring big on *la tierce* or another combination—there is also *une quarte,* a four-horse combination played mid-week—are miniscule. The winners usually include at least one or two horses totally ignored by the prognostics. But this is nothing new in racing.

The wisest course is to place 50 francs on 10 well-considered but partly arbitrary combinations, go to the track, and enjoy the day. Placing a few on-track bets heightens the interest, but for the casual visitor the greatest pleasure is watching the horses and the jockeys and taking in the atmosphere.

Radio Days

Another feature of the 16th is the Radio House (la Maison de la RTF, or Radio Télévision Français). This unusual construction consists of a round building rising from 6 stories in front to 10 stories in the rear and circling a shaft-like tower.

Nearby, at 55 Carre du Dr. Blanche, is a small museum funded by the Corbusier Foundation. Two connected villas house the plans of le Corbusier's various buildings. The villas are furnished and worth a visit for anyone interested in architecture. The museum is open Monday through Friday, 10 a.m. to 12:45 p.m. and 2 p.m. to 6 p.m. It is closed in August. The entry fee is FF5.

The Other "Villages"

Passy was a village some distance from Paris when Benjamin Franklin lived here. He stayed in the former l'Hôtel de Valentinois that was at 62 and 66 rue Raynouard. Here he received all the Americans then in Paris, as well as the most distinguished men in France. He made his first experiment here with a lightning rod, and his host allowed him to set up a printing press in one of the outbuildings on the property. It was also in Passy that Pilatre de Rozier and the Marquis d'Arlandes launched the first man-bearing free-flight balloon in 1783. Benjamin Franklin was among the witnesses watching the first men to leave the planet soar over the Seine for a 25-minute flight.

Balzac also lived in Passy, and his dwelling at 47 rue Raynouard has been preserved. It is now a museum.

The Passy hillside facing south once produced grapes for wine. There is *un musée du vin* (wine museum) incredibly located on la rue des Eaux (Water Street) on la place Dickens. It is worth a visit if only for a view of the medieval cellars, and the entrance fee (FF20) includes a taste of wine. It is closed Monday but open other days from 2 p.m. to 6 p.m.

Le Trocadéro is the most interesting square of the 16th. The seldom-visited Musée des Monuments Français (open daily from 10 a.m. to 7 p.m. except Tuesday) exhibits copies of frescoes, stonework, architectural sculpture, and murals from all parts of France. The collection dates from the 12th century.

Another often overlooked museum is le Musée Guimet on la place d'Iena (open 9:45 a.m. to noon and 1:30 p.m. to 5:15 p.m. except Tuesday). This houses one of the largest collections of Asiatic bronzes, ivories, furniture, jewels, and ceramics in the Western World.

Look at one of the weekly magazines—*Pariscope* or *l'Officiel des Spectacles*—for news of exhibits at le Musée d'Art Moderne de la Ville de Paris. This modern-art museum is in a building called le Palais de Tokyo, 11 ave. du President Wilson. There are exceptionally interesting photo exhibits here all year. The permanent collection of 20th-century art is also worth a visit.

On the other side of le Trocadéro area, on a pleasant tree-lined urban square called le Jardin de Ranelagh, the little Musée Marmottan is established in a beautiful mansion. It is the former home of the art historian Paul Marmottan. This collection of works by Impressionists, mainly 65 paintings by Claude Monet, is special. The museum is open daily 10 a.m. to 6 p.m. except Monday.

The part of the 16th nearest l'Etoile (or la place General de Gaulle, as it is now called) is strictly residential. But *les grand maisons* along l'avenue Foch are quite impressive. And a stroll along l'avenue Victor Hugo is a window-shopping experience often overlooked by visitors. While there you might want to try the wonderful old fish restaurant, Prunier Traktir, at number 16. It's expensive but a real Paris treat.

Le Bois de Boulogne is a 2,100-acre park with 163 acres of grasslands, 66 acres of playgrounds and sports fields, 241 acres of roadways, 73 acres of lakes, 24 miles of roads open to automobile traffic, 6 miles of roads for walking, 624 acres of woods, and 206 acres of gardens. Nearly 150 gardeners work full-time on maintenance. There are two race tracks (Auteuil and Longchamp), a children's park (le Jardin d'Acclimatation), a museum of popular arts and traditions, and one of the world's greatest rose gardens, la Bagatelle. There are elegant and expensive restaurants in le Bois as well as modest lunchrooms and picnic facilities. You can rent row boats at the lake, and there is an island to explore.

Little public transportation exists in le Bois itself. It is best to go by metro to la Porte Dauphine or la Porte Maillot or by bus to la Porte Muette (No. 63) or la Porte Passy (No. 32). One bus (No. 334 from la Porte Maillot) takes you through *le bois* to the Longchamp race track. Walking or cycling is best, however, and bicycles can be

51

rented from March to the end of November at 8 place de la Porte
Champerret, 17th.

Savoring the Past

The 17th is not as chic as the 16th, nor does it have much in the
way of monuments or tourist attractions. Yet it has a very special
flavor of Paris as it must have been in the first years of this century.
The streets are wide and for the most part neatly squared, signs of the
work of Haussmann. The buildings are of uniform height and sym-
metrically designed with only a few present-day defacements.

The 17th became a part of Paris when the city incorporated the
community of Batignolles in 1860. The entire section appears to have
been built between 1850 and 1914 in the Haussmann style. Aside
from some interesting houses on a few streets such as Tocqueville or
Ampere, most follow the same pattern. A late addition (1904) is the
Ceramic Hotel at 32 ave. Wagram. It has an interesting *art nouveau*
sandstone front. Also unique is la Cité des Fleurs (154 ave. de
Clichy), where little two- to three-story houses with private gardens
provide a bucolic interlude.

Near the corner of la rue de Courcelles and l'avenue de Courcelles,
on the small rue de Chazelle, is the warehouse where the Statue of
Liberty was constructed and assembled before shipping. For a short
time the statue loomed 151 feet above street level, towering over the
surrounding buildings.

Recommended Restaurants

Many of the good and interesting eating places in these two
arrondissements are highly rated in the Paris restaurant guides (a total
of 37 *Michelin* stars are awarded in the 16th and 17th).

Below is a handful that deserve more credit than they get in the
guides.

Chez Georges, 273 blvd. Pereire, 17th; tel. 45.74.31.00. Open
every day; closed August. One of those old Paris establishments
founded in the 1930s and taken over by a son practically without
change. This place is devoted to the great meat dishes of French cuisine: *navarin de mouton, le petit salé, gigot d'agneau,* and roast beef.
The potatoes *gratin dauphinoise* are as good as any in all France. Fun
desserts. About FF250.

Chez la Mère Michel, 5 rue Rennequin, 17th; tel. 47.63.
59.80. Closed Saturday, Sunday, and holidays. Until a few years ago
there actually was a Mère Michel. The muscles of her right arm were
highly developed from beating butter, and her *beurre blanc* was justly

renowned. Monsieur Bernard Gaillard, who took over upon Mère Michel's retirement, has maintained the specialties: *coquilles Saint-Jacques, saumon grillé*, sea fish, and *brochet* (pike)—all with *beurre blanc*—and has gained for himself the reputation that Mère Michel once enjoyed. About FF250.

Paul Chene, 123 rue Lauriston, 16th; tel. 47.27.63.17. Closed Saturday and Sunday. An excellent eating place run by a man who knows good food and how to prepare it. Fish soup with *une rouille,* veal kidneys with three mustards, rabbit in a jelly made with reisling wine, *un boeuf daube á l'ancienne, poule au pot Henri IV,* and many other strictly French dishes. More than FF300.

Prunier Traktir, 16 ave. Victor Hugo, 16th; tel. 45.00. 89.12. Closed Monday and Tuesday, except during July and August when closed Sunday and Monday. There has been a Prunier restaurant in Paris since 1925. Then and now it specializes in good seafood. This is one of the fine old restaurants of Paris. More than FF300.

Ramponneau, 21 ave. Marceau, 16th; tel. 47.20.59.51. Open daily; closed August. The atmosphere in this elegant but under-decorated fine old restaurant (it was here in the 1920s) is worth the price. The food has for many years been underrated by all the guides. The grilled salmon with a mustard sauce, the grilled *andouillettes, le poule-au-pot,* the rabbit with chestnuts, and the duck liver with grapes are very good and professionally served. About FF300.

The 18th, 19th, and 20th *Arrondissements*

The history and the legend of la Mont des Martyrs (known in Roman times as the Mons Martyrum) are well-told in the *Michelin Green Guide.*

In the beginning of the 19th century, the rustic butte Montmartre was still a village of gardens, vineyards, farmhouses, and 40-odd windmills with a population of 638 chalk miners and stone-quarry laborers. Many Parisians, evicted when Haussmann tore down hundreds of old houses in the city center, chose to resettle on the heights. Rents were low. And the wine made here was not subject to tax, as it did not have to pass the "wall of the tax collectors" that surrounded Paris. In 1860, along with a number of other outlying villages, Montmartre was annexed to Paris.

Nonetheless, for many years at the end of the 19th and beginning of the 20th centuries, Montmartre remained a village beautifully documented by Utrillo, Sisley, Pissarro, Van Gogh, and so many others. The ambiance lasted until the first decade of the 20th century.

Montmartre—la rue Saint-Vincent.

Most of those who live in Montmartre today have no desire to move. They are fiercely loyal to what they like to think of as the "Republic of Montmartre." They still maintain a vineyard and make wine each year, they have their own museum, and there is even a wax museum depicting the important historic events of the "republic." The masses of tourists that constantly pour through the narrow streets seem not to bother the locals any more than the weather. To them the tourism is a phenomenon, and aside from providing a living for some of the residents, it has little to do with life on the butte.

On the very top of Montmartre, next to la place du Tertre, is one of the oldest churches in Paris. **Saint-Pierre de Montmartre** (constructed in 1134) is the last trace of the Abbey of Montmartre. This charming little church was built on the site of a Gallo-Roman temple, evidence of which can be found in the two decorative columns built into the entrance way of the church. It became the chapel of a convent for noble ladies until the Revolution. A cemetery next to the church dates back to the Merovingian kings. Unfortunately, the church is only open one day a year—Nov. 1 (All Saints Day).

L'avenue Junot, the most expensive street in Montmartre, is lined with beautiful trees. The rather good houses on either side have gardens with vegetable plots. Many even have chicken coops, and some inhabitants raise goats. A few of the houses are 1920s art-deco, but the rest date from the last century or before. At the end of the street is the little cemetery Saint-Vincent, where Utrillo is buried.

The **Montmartre vineyard** can be found at the corner of la rue Saint-Vincent and la rue des Saules, near the Montmartre Museum. This is a pleasant spot. The museum is in a wonderful old house on top of the slope, and the vineyard seems to surround it. The vines still produce a wine called picolo. Every autumn, usually the first Sunday in October, when all the grapes are in, there is **une Fête des Vendanges** at the vineyard. The more than 300 liters of wine produced are sold and the proceeds given to the old people who live on the butte.

Artists in Montmartre

Renoir was among many 19th-century artists who lived in Montmartre and loved it. When traveling in Italy in 1881 he wrote from Naples:

"I feel a little lost when away from Montmartre...I am longing for my familiar surroundings and think that even the ugliest girl is preferable to the most beautiful Italian."

A large garden, actually an abandoned park, is behind Renoir's house on la rue Cortot. It gave the artist ample opportunity to paint in the open air (see *La Balançoire* at le Musée d'Orsay).

At 18 rue Saint-Rustique there is a plaque on a house that was famous during the last half of the 19th century. Called *Aux Billards en Bois,* it was the meeting place for Diaz, Pissarro, Degas, Sisley, Cezanne, Lautrec, Renoir, Monet, and Emile Zola. In October 1886, Van Gogh painted his masterpiece *La Guinguette* (now at the Louvre) using this garden as a background.

From la place d'Anvers on le boulevard de Rochechouart, la rue Steinkerque leads to la place and le marché Saint-Pierre directly below le Sacré Coeur. Odds and ends of cloth are sold in the various shops along the street. A new and interesting museum, l'Halle Saint-Pierre (1 rue Ronsard), once a fabric market, has temporary exhibits and a permanent collection of naive paintings. It also houses a children's museum. The building is an old Baltard iron and glass "hangar," newly refurbished inside with wooden floors and stairways.

Strip Tease

"God created the world, Napoléon founded la Légion d'Honneur, and I have established Montmartre," claimed Rodolphe Salis. And he described it thus:

"Montmartre, the city of Freedom, sacred hillock, salt of the earth, navel and nerve center of the world, breast of granite at which successive generations athirst for an ideal come to slake their thirst!"

Salis founded le Chat Noir, the first *cabaret artistique* in Montmartre. It was at 84 blvd. de Rochechouart, a few doors from la place Pigalle.

It was in this neighborhood that Paris acquired its reputation as "Gay Paree." Today, la place Pigalle, a tawdry square with night entertainment of little interest, still rides on its old reputation. Even at

55

the end of the 18th century, when the village of Montmartre was a peaceful rural spot, 25 of the 58 houses on la rue Montmartre were cabarets. A century later the artistic and literary *cafés* dominated the scene. Le Chat Noir, made famous by Toulouse Lautrec's posters, featured the singer Aristide Bruant. His songs had their roots in the slangy language of the Parisian working class. They expressed much of the suffering, anxiety, and instinctive rebelliousness of the poor, who lived just north and east of Paris, where the 18th, 19th, and 20th *arrondissements* are today.

Aside from the drug traffic, prostitution, and tatoo parlors of today, however, the night life is beginning to show signs of a renaissance. New faces are appearing on stage, new customers in the audiences.

Below are a few places that have shown enough improvement to warrant a recommendation. There's something for just about everybody, but undoubtedly some will find none of the fare to their taste. Note that the 9th *arrondissement* borders on the 18th at Pigalle, thus many addresses just off the boulevard are in the 9th.

Le Martial, 26 rue Fontaine, 9th; tel. 42.80.04.57. Open every night from 10 p.m. to 6 a.m. The minimum check is FF70. Musicians, magicians, and a strip tease. The show is different every night (but always "very modern").

La Nouvelle Eve, 25 rue Fontaine, 9th; tel. 45.26.68.18. Open Friday night starting at 11 p.m. The entrance fee is FF100. The meeting place once a week for Paris' answer to preppies—the BCBG (*les bon chic, bon gens*).

La Locomotive, 90 blvd. de Clichy, 18th; tel. 42.64.39.42. Open every day except Monday. Private parties. The entry fee is FF50 weekdays and FF80 weekends. The biggest "rock" on the new Paris scene. The decoration is completely wild.

French Lovers, 62 rue Pigalle, 9th; tel. 42.85.32.69. Open 2 p.m. to midnight except Sunday. The entry fee is FF250. Live sex, pure and simple.

La Cloche, 3 rue Mansart, 9th; tel. 48.74.44.88. Open every day except Sunday until 2 a.m. An atmosphere of rustic Normandy. The audiences from nearby theaters come here for *un pot-au-feu* and grilled *andouillette*. About FF150. (While in the neighborhood be sure to visit the interesting and most unusual Musée Gustave Moreau, 14 rue de la Rochefoucault.)

The Enclaves

Almost directly north of Paris, a little square of land once contained fruitful vineyards that produced a fine, golden white wine that earned the title *la Goutte d'Or* (Drop of Gold). **La Goutte d'Or,** as the area is now known, is still inhabited by fiercely independent people who remain apart from their neighbors. Unfortunately, it is scheduled for "modernization" by the city government. Visit it while you still can.

Ironically, it was demolition that created la Goutte d'Or and the other once-small towns that swelled with Parisians forced out of the city center in the 19th century. When Haussmann cleared many slum areas on the narrow winding streets in the center of town, most of those who were displaced moved to the east of the city. Here Haussmann had done little more than build some access roads from the center of Paris.

The 19th and 20th *arrondissements* were made a part of Paris in 1840. The area they comprise includes two small towns, Charonne and Belleville, as well as the hamlet called **Menilmontant.** This curious name existed in the 13th century as "Mesnil-mau-temps," a "small farm (or hamlet) of the bad times." Some etymologists, however, say the town was originally "Mesnil-montant" ("hamlet on the hill"), because the village was situated on an escarpment overlooking Paris.

This escarpment, where today the cemetery Père Lachaise is located, was known as le Champ de l'Evêque (Bishop's Field) in the 12th century. It was the property of the bishop of Paris. Here he grew vegetables, wheat, and grapes that were then stored in the larder attached to the Notre Dame chapel.

The land was bought in the 15th century by a rich spice merchant named Regnault de Wandonne, who built his country house, la Folie-Regnault, on the site in 1430. At that time, the word *folie* did not have the connotation of "folly" as it does now but simply meant Regnault's "place."

In the 17th century, a teaching order of Jesuits, established on la rue Saint-Antoine, acquired the land and built a rest and convalescent home on the crest of the hill. The place was then called Mont-Louis.

The Jesuits presented the house to Father François la Chaise d'Aix when he became confessor to Louis XIV. Père la Chaise, in his position as confessor, had considerable influence with the king. He became very popular with Parisian courtesans, many of whom began to spend a great deal of time with him.

When the Jesuits were expelled from France in 1763, the land was left to a person called Gratin. In 1771, the land became the collective property of a family named Baron who, when ruined by the Revolution, sold the property to the city of Paris.

The property was to be used as one of the three cemeteries the city of Paris was setting up *intra-muros*. Père Lachaise, as this cemetery is now known, was enlarged several times during the next 100 years, becoming the largest in Paris. It was, until 1824, the only city cemetery authorized to grant permanent concessions. There are many famous people interred in Père Lachaise, but the senior citizens are Heloise and Abelard, who after several separate reburials were finally united in 1817 in a single grave.

When these communes outside Paris were still villages, Parisians traditionally spent their Sundays on the heights. Here cabarets, dance halls, and pubs prospered. Menilmontant, until the turn of the century, produced a simple red wine that, like the other wines produced in the Paris suburbs, was not taxed if drunk at the vineyard. The wine and the visiting Parisians inspired local singing poets, who developed a lively, sharp wit.

Belleville was another village that mushroomed under an influx of working-class Parisians. Edith Giovanna Gassion, who became internationally famous as Edith Piaf, was born here. Her songs, defiant and sentimental, reflected the character of Belleville's inhabitants.

Belleville, like other small communities on the outskirts of the city, had the reputation of being a hot spot in revolts and uprisings. In the mid-19th century, it was annexed to Paris. Haussmann was careful to have Belleville straddle the line between two *arrondissements*, depriving it of administrative power as a unit.

The growing population of low- and middle-income workers meant a desperate need for new, inexpensive housing in these *arrondissements*. Government housing was then unheard of, but a private society was organized to build low-cost housing. La Société Française des Habitations á Bon Marché (HBM) was created in 1885. It was 39 years later, in 1928, that the government first participated directly in low-cost housing projects.

A good example of private low-cost housing from that early era is the **Campagne á Paris** (Countrified Paris). It is a complex of 92 bungalows built in 1908 for families of civil servants, bank employees, and other lower- to middle-income workers. The houses were financed on a sort of "lend-lease" arrangement, in which the purchaser was given some credit toward purchase through monthly payments. Built of excellent materials, surrounded by abundant greenery, and decorated with amusing details (each of the 92 was designed by a different architect, or built without an architect), they are still in excellent shape and highly prized today. Although the original plan of creating a countrified environment did not quite come off, the aroma of lilac in spring is overwhelming.

There is a stairway leading to Campagne á Paris from la rue Geo-Chavez (leads off la place de la Porte de Bagnolet to la rue Belgrand). The houses are on la rue Irenee Blanc, la rue Jules-Siegfried, la rue Paul-Strauss, and la rue Captain Ferber (the latter was a French-born American aviation pioneer).

Another interesting experiment was the so-called "fortresses" built in this part of town at about the same time. In an attempt to provide convenience and security, several complexes were built as *une ville dans une ville,* or a city within a city. These usually had gates leading to a central court that provided access to the apartments and contained communal facilities to make the tenants as independent of the rest of the city as possible. An example of this type of structure can be seen at 5 rue Ernest-Lefèvre.

Brick, an economic building material at the beginning of the 20th century, characterizes low-cost housing of the epoch. It is often used decoratively with tile. Today brick still marks contemporary low-cost construction, and because of the lack of comfort in many of the early HBM buildings, it has also become a symbol of bad housing.

An example of a fortress-like structure with remarkable brickwork can be seen at 40 rue de Menilmontant.

Recommended Restaurants

Most of the recommended restaurants in this part of town are either in Montmartre or Villette, the site of the old slaughterhouses. The *Michelin* guide finds only 18 worth mention, but the *Gault and Millau* squeezes out 32. Here are seven:

Le Sancerre, 13 ave. Corentin-Cariou, 19th; tel. 46.07.80.44. Closed Saturday and Sunday. A *bistrot*-type restaurant with a long bar *(un zinc).* Very old-fashioned. Once we had terrific *frites* (french fries), the next time they were terrible. But on the whole this is a good, inexpensive place for lunch, especially if you are spending the day at the Villette Museum. About FF190.

A la Pomponnette, 42 rue Lepic, 18th; tel. 46.06.08.36. Closed Sunday night, Monday, and August. A typical Montmartre neighborhood restaurant. Good food, a bit expensive. FF180.

Au Cochon d'Or, 192 ave. Jean-Jaures, 19th; tel. 46.07.23.13. Open every day. At one time, when the stockyards were just across the street, this place and about six others were "the" places to go in Paris for good steak. Unlike any other place in town, the steaks were cut thick. There are only a few of these restaurants left here—this and one or two others. Maybe they will revive when the Villette City of Science in the old slaughterhouse is operating in full swing. Meantime le Cochon d'Or is still the place for an extraordinary steak. About FF320.

Au Bistrot du Port, 50 Quai de la Loire, 19th; tel. 46.70. 43.96. Closed Saturday and Sunday. This is at the end of the canal trip. The boat drops you here at lunch time, and it's a nice place to eat. Very much the local place. Very simple, good French food. About FF130.

Charlot 1er, 128*bis* blvd. de Clichy, 18th; tel. 45.22.47.08. Closed July 14 to Aug. 23. This is probably the best (not by any means the least expensive) place for good fresh fish in Paris. About FF350, depending on your tastes.

(Across the street in the 9th *arrondissement* is another big fish restaurant also called Charlot. It is owned by a family who seems to be intent on getting control of a large number of restaurants catering to large numbers of people.)

Chez Roger, 145 rue d'Avron, 20th; tel. 43.73.55.47. Closed Wednesday night and Thursday; serves only until 8:30 p.m. A happy *bistrot*, with red-checked napkins and tablecloths. An old-fashioned bill of fare with *céleri rémoulade*, hard-boiled eggs with mayonnaise, marinated herring, *gigot* with *flageolets*, *boudin*, etc. One must eat these often to remember how very good they are. About FF100.

Le Boeuf Bourguignon, 21 rue de Douai, 19th; tel. 42.82. 08.79. Closed Sunday; serves until 10 p.m. Don't expect comfort or ambiance. The lighting is cruel and the chairs uncomfortable, but the food is superb. This is where television, radio, and film people go to eat, not to be seen or to look at each other. *Un menu* (fixed-price meal) is FF49.50, including three courses and a carafe of wine. *A la carte* is less than FF100 with a good wine.

La Défense

Because Parisians made a heroic stand on this site during the Siege of 1870, it is known today as la Défense. Formerly it was known as la Butte Chantecoq. La Défense is not part of Paris, but it is part of the view from almost any section. That's either a pleasure or an irritation, depending on how you feel about high-rises. The best view of la Défense is from the terrace of *le pavillon* at Saint-Germain-en-Laye (nine miles from la Porte Maillot, seven miles from la Défense).

During the past 20 years, this hilltop has undergone a fantastic change, from a sleepy suburb to a 2,000-acre cement and stone city of towers rising up to 45 stories. It is divided into business and residential areas. About 30,000 people live here, and another 55,000 come to work here daily.

Several-dozen nationalities live together in quarters that are neither expensive nor exclusive (but there is not any really low-cost housing either). On weekends roller skating and wind sailing are possible in the residential section as well as on the esplanade in front of the commercial center. The commercial center has 215 shops, including two discount houses and nine movie houses (seldom crowded). There are 40-odd restaurants and bars, 8 indoor tennis courts, and 9 squash courts. La Défense is only four minutes by RER from l'Arc de Triomphe. The air is pure, and it's quiet at night and well-lit.

If you go, be sure to see the statue commemorating the Seize of 1870. It was erected by the Third Republic, which held an open competition for an appropriate statue. Rodin and Gustave Dore presented their projects, but it was that of unknown Louis Ernest Barrias that was finally selected. The composition is largely allegoric: The city of Paris is a female dressed in the coat of *une garde mobile*, saving the flag while protecting the unfortunate people of Paris, symbolized by a little girl.

The statue was placed at le Rond Point de la Défense in 1871, then moved during the 1960s while the high-rise construction was under way. It was replaced at its original site in 1983.

Chinatown

There has been a steady decline in the numbers of artisans, shopkeepers, and workers in Paris—a favorable condition for immigration. As the Parisians leave, foreigners come in. Twenty years ago, except for some North African restaurants, there were almost no ethnic places to eat in Paris. However, a recent estimate gave more than 100 Asian restaurants in the 13th *arrondissement* alone. Asian restaurants are now seen in all parts of Paris.

Approximately 400,000 foreigners live in Paris. Most are from Algeria (65,000), Portugal (45,000), Spain and Tunisia (30,000 each), Morocco (25,000), and Yugoslavia and Italy (15,000 each). The rest fall into the refugee category: Cambodians (7,500), Vietnamese (4,000), Laotians (2,000), Poles (2,000), and Russians (1,000).

The "Yellow Triangle," the largest Chinatown in Europe, is around la place d'Italie in the southern part of Paris. In the 1960s, a dozen or more high-rises were built, and since then 5,000 Asians have taken refuge here. Although they are classified as Cambodians, Laotians, and Vietnamse, almost all are part of the Chinese diaspora of Southeast Asia. An apparently uniform community, with Mandarin as its official language, there is great diversity of dialect, religion, and culture. Nevertheless, the sense of being Chinese is very important. "At last, here on the banks of the Seine, we have created the traditional China," wrote Mlle Yuan, editor of a bimonthly Chinese magazine published in Paris.

The Asians are not confined to Paris, however. In three years, Belleville has changed its color. Once Arab and Jewish, today it is almost all Asian owned and operated. There is a large Asian population in la place de Torcy in the 18th *arrondissement* and in the suburbs of Vitry, Noisy-le-Grand, Lognes, and Ivry. Restaurants, grocery stores, fast-food shops, supermarkets, hi-fi and television boutiques, and travel agencies have changed hands, too. The Asian refugees move in quickly, make exceptionally high offers for neighborhood businesses, and take them over.

A much older Chinese enclave of 6,000 or 7,000 lives quietly in le Marais between rue au Maire, rue des Gravilliers, and rue du Temple. This is the third largest Asian colony in Paris. There are no obvious signs or Chinese names, but the smell of lacquered duck drifting down any one of the streets is a quick tip-off. This enclave has existed for nearly 70 years, since the French government accepted 100,000 immigrants from the young republic of Sun Yat Sen to replace workers who had gone to fight in World War I. Some among them later became famous—Chou En Lai and Den Xiaoping, for example. When the war was over, many of those from northern China remained in Paris to settle in the 3rd *arrondissement*, specializing in leatherwork and garment manufacturing. Today the government has accepted some southern Chinese from the province of Wenshou, near Shanghai.

If you keep your eyes open as you walk through this enclave, you will discover many signs of the community. Go into le Cours de Rome and to Chez Ton, 37 rue au Maire, one of the least expensive restaurants in all Paris—FF31, everything included!

Unlike the New York and San Francisco Chinatowns, these ethnic clusters are not exotic in architecture or the dress of people on the streets. The Asians look very Western. Even restaurants tend to refrain from emphasizing oriental decoration, which was once their stock in trade.

The pattern for success is much the same as in American Asian enclaves. The Orientals, often illegally in France, work 12 to 14 hours a day without compensation for overtime, vacations, or other amenities demanded by the French. They live frugally and save money by living 12 or 14 to a two-bedroom apartment.

Loans are made available using the same system known in San Francisco's Chinatown at the turn of the century. A group pools its savings, then each potential borrower writes on a scrap of paper how much interest he is willing to pay. The highest bidder gets the loan, thus generating interest rates as high as 30%. Once established in business, a family puts in all its efforts and capital to expand. These businesses are created and grow with no papers signed and no legal recourse but with total confidence. The pools, often made up of as many as 3,000 members, start with considerable cash assets, even though some contribute as little as FF1,000.

Once in possession of the money, there are no taxes, lawyers' fees, or time lost with contracts; the entrepreneur is in business. The French authorities try to limit Chinese solidarity to some extent, but this has only forced many businesses underground. As the businesses get bigger, though, they usually become "legal."

A Guide to Buying Real Estate in Paris
A Little History

In the Middle Ages, Paris houses were built with the ground floor of cut stone supporting a frame of wooden beams. The interstices between the beams were filled with scrap stone and plaster of paris, usually leaving the facing surface of the beams exposed. Called colombage, this construction was forbidden in 1560, because it was a fire hazard. One example still exists at 3 rue Volta, 3rd. It's probably the oldest house in Paris.

Cantilevered houses that had upper floors projecting out over the street were another typical medieval design. These afforded pedestrians protection from the rain but created very dark and dangerous streets. In 1607 these, too, were outlawed.

Until the Renaissance, the houses of Paris were all gabled, with the narrow side toward the street. This created a saw-toothed roof line. Today, there are only about 30 of these houses left in Paris.

Before the mid-17th century, the height of houses was limited to 50 or 60 feet. But as the population grew, stories were added. By the end of the 18th century 8 houses in 10 in the center of Paris were 4 to 7 stories high. A relationship between the height of houses and the width of the street was fixed by decrees in 1783 and 1902.

Paris Real Estate Today

In 1850 Napoléon III and his prefect of Paris, Georges Haussmann, tore the city apart to construct boulevards, new streets, public buildings, and parks. Private contractors snapped up the vacant lots left by the reconstruction and built houses by the score.

The typical structure put up by private builders was an apartment building six or seven stories tall. The ground floor was commonly occupied by shops and a prominent entrance way that was usually wide enough to admit a carriage. The entrance led through a passage and into an inner court. There stairways led to apartments on the floors above. The government required buyers to erect buildings with facades conforming to plans prescribed by the city, so there's a somewhat uniform appearance to buildings erected during this period. Balconies with wrought-iron railings set off the windows in the facades, and a continuous iron railing crowned the cornice. Ornamental stonework—caryatids and consoles—supported balconies; the windows featured sculptured reliefs; and decorative medallions adorned most buildings.

On any one street the buildings were generally about the same height, for the law fixed a maximum number of floors that varied with the width of the streets. Owners, wanting the largest possible return, built to the maximum. Often they added an extra rentable story above the cornice line by having a mansard roof with dormer windows opening into rooms immediately under the roof timbers.

The regulations also enforced maintenance standards for all buildings, new and old. An 1852 decree required proprietors to clean or repaint facades at least once every 10 years. DeGaulle and Malraux applied this still-existing ordinance in 1959, when they ordered that all Paris buildings be cleaned after many years of neglect.

Hundreds of these buildings still stand in Paris today. But most have been chopped into smaller and more practical units or modernized, with central heating, bathrooms, and improved kitchens.

The ceilings are high and the hallways wide, but the floor plan is almost invariably impractical. The large multiroom apartments, filling an entire floor, were designed for families with one or more servants; often the kitchen was on the opposite side of the court and accessible only down a long corridor.

Haussmann-period mansions and those that are older have been sold floor by floor for the past 25 years. It is these that are on the market from time to time today for a fortune or a song, for better or worse. Some are sold "to be modernized," for which one has to add to the purchase price at least $42 a square foot.

Except for almost the entire eastern part of Paris (11th, 12th, 18th, 19th, and 20th *arrondissements*), the real estate agents have gleaned the best and sold and resold them. Although the cost per square foot varies in each sector, the average in those most in demand (6th, 7th, 16th, and 17th *arrondissements*, le Marais, l'Ile Saint-Louis, and les Champs-Elysées) is very high.

Prices jump with changes in the neighborhood. The opening of the Picasso museum, for example, doubled the prices on la rue Thorigny.

In the neighborhood of les Halles (the old food market, now a super shopping mall, cultural center, and strolling area), prices soared when it was renovated.

In the workingmen's quarters of the 18th, 19th, and 20th *arrondissements*, prices almost never go above $100 a square foot and are usually about half that. They start to creep up in the 11th and 12th *arrondissements*, where the average runs from $100 to $116 a square foot. The exceptions in these pricier parts of town are such off-beat locations as the tree-lined boulevard Beaumarchais in the 11th, along le Quai Valmy on le Canal Saint-Martin, around le Parc des Buttes Chaumont in the 19th, and on l'avenue Junot in the 18th.

For an apartment in high-toned areas, such as l'avenue Henri-Martin, le Trocadéro, and la Porte de la Muette, prices range from $245 to as much as $315 a square foot. In the highly esteemed Left Bank areas of the 6th and 7th *arrondissements* or around le Parc Monceau in the 17th, prices jump to more than $285 and even up to $360 a square foot.

Seldom available, but also highly prized, are apartments on l'Ile Saint-Louis, in la place des Vosges, and in the neighborhood of le Pantheon, where $430 a square foot is not unusual. Still higher ($470 to $500 a square foot) is space around the greenery of le Champ-de-Mars, the area facing le Jardin de Luxembourg (on la rue Guynemer), the wooded area near la Muette, and the charming place Furstenburg.

The high price of greenery is evident in the $430 to $570 a square foot one has to pay for apartments on l'avenue Raphael along le Jardin du Ranelagh and for those that face le Bois de Boulogne in Neuilly.

These figures are, of course, average; in any section of town prices can vary from 30% to 50% from one street to another, from one side of a street to the other, and from floor to floor in the same house. The ground floor sells for an average of 15% to 30% less than upper floors. Busy or noisy streets, such as la rue de la Huchette, where the smell of Merguez sausages is overwhelming, and those with junk food shops are obviously less expensive than other streets in the same neighborhoods.

For a real bargain, though, take a look at a loft. Parisians have only recently discovered the possibilities of the loft as a lodging place. Two years ago, unfurnished lofts around the Bastille were selling for as little as $70 a square foot. Today, few remain, and those that are for sale have doubled in price. The French *bourgeois*, while fascinated with the space offered by a loft, do not like the often crude entryways and commercial addresses. Thus lofts are being snatched up by foreigners, especially Americans, who recognize their potential.

Note that only 8% of the lodging space left in Paris is larger than 100 square meters, making it difficult for families to live in town. About 58% of available apartments are studio or two-room.

La Salpêtrière—place et rue du Conseli.

Chapter III

Finding French C

As you might expect, a city and country noted for its cooking must have fine food markets. Until 1969 the Paris daily wholesale food market, les Halles, was in the center of the city. (It had been established in that location during the ninth century; then it was outside the city walls.) Today it is once again outside town west of Paris near Orly airport. The area is restricted to people with buyer cards, and it is so well-arranged that it is totally uninteresting. Unlike the old Halles, where one could go for onion soup in the small hours of the morning and where one had many excellent restaurants to choose from, the new market's amenities are sparse. Today's chefs, retailers, and buyers do not remain here an instant longer than necessary.

The Covered Markets of Paris

Fortunately, there are still a few traditional covered markets in Paris. If you enjoy food and eating you will appreciate their displays of seasonal fresh fruit and vegetables, meat and cheese. The stacked mushrooms and melons, the presentation of the many cheeses, the perfect symmetry of well-cut pieces of fresh meat, and the fall and winter displays of furred and feathered game—hare, deer, boar, wild duck, pigeon, partridge, pheasant, quail—are a mouth-watering pleasure to see.

There are 12 covered markets still operating in Paris. Enjoy them while you can—they probably won't be around for long. The government, for some undisclosed reason, seems to support the anonymous packages of food that come from no one knows where and are sold by vendors with little or no knowledge of their wares.

The remaining covered markets in Paris include:

Enfants Rouge, 39 rue de Bretagne, 3rd.

Saint-Germain, between rues Lobineau, Clement, and Mabillon, 6th.

Porte Saint-Martin, 31 and 33 rue du Château-d'Eau, 10th.

Saint-Quentin, 85*bis* blvd. Magenta, 10th.

Beauvau Saint-Antoine, between rues d'Aligre and de Cotte, 12th.

The Saint-Germain market.

Passy, corner of rues Bois-le-Vent and Duban, 16th.

Saint-Didier, corner of rues Mesnil and Saint-Didier, 16th (both covered and open street markets plus boutiques).

Batignolles, 96 rue Lemercier, 17th.

Ternes, rues Lebon, Faraday, and Torricelli, 17th.

La Chapelle, rue de l'Olive, 18th (open until midnight on Friday and Saturday).

Riquet, 36 and 46 rue Riquet, 18th (open until 8 p.m. on Friday and Saturday).

Secretan, 46 rue Bouret and 33 ave. Secretan, 19th.

At an Open Street Market

Open street markets are also declining in number, but more slowly. There are 55 still operating in Paris. Each sets up and is ready for business by 7:30 a.m., folding and disappearing at 1:30 p.m. regularly two or three times a week (never on Mondays).

It's worth the time and effort to be on hand early when these markets set up. Metal tubes are placed in holes in the pavement, then a canvas is unrolled over the tubes to create a protective roof on each stand. The trucks arrive, slowly at first, one at a time. Then as the opening hour draws close, three, four, and even more maneuver simultaneously for a place to park. They begin to unload almost before the truck's motor has died. Out come long flat boxes of fresh farm cheeses, crates of red, green, and yellow apples, and little baskets of fragrant strawberries or raspberries in season. Great bunches of wildly colored fresh flowers, whole hams, and strings of sausage, carrying a pungent wood-smoke smell, are hung, while across the aisle are trays of glistening, silvery fresh fish smelling of the sea.

For a brief moment the bustle dies, as most of the vendors have stacked, hung, arranged, piled, or spread their wares. A few disappear for coffee in a nearby cafe. Then almost before an observer is fully conscious of the lack of bustle and noise, the customers begin to arrive. The crescendo builds as the vendors shout their boasts, and customers and sellers carry on what seems a constant conversation about the quality of the food. Milling buyers fill their deep market bags with the makings of several days' meals.

The movement and din continue without let up until the clock nears 1:30 p.m. Then the crowd thins, and the merchants begin to pick up the leftovers, pack them ready to be carried in the proper order, and place them carefully back in the trucks. Much in the same manner as they arrived, the trucks depart: the doors slam, and first one or two at a time, then in larger numbers they roll away leaving a few stragglers among the terrible mess of paper, broken wooden crates, plastic and cardboard boxes, damaged baskets, carrot and beet tops, cabbage leaves, and bits of overripe fruits and vegetables.

In less than an hour the crew who brought the poles and canvas are on hand to dismantle the temporary shopping center. When all the poles are back in the trucks along with the rolled canvas tops, the street-cleaning crew arrives with hoses and brooms, sweeping and washing everything into neat piles of waste and trash ready to be loaded onto the garbage collection trucks. Like the manipulators of the tent poles, they too work with a swift precision. When finished they roll away, their broomsticks protruding from the trucks like empty flagpoles or the spears of a dozen crusaders, leaving the street clean and glistening in the afternoon sunshine.

With a camera, a witness could spend a profitable half-day photographing the phases of *un marché* from the setting up of the poles to the cleaning of the street after the market closes.

More than 50 street markets are operating in Paris. Here is a list of a few:

Carmes, place Maubert, 5th; Tuesday, Thursday, and Saturday.

Port-Royal de Paris, along the wall of l'hôpital Val-de-Grâce, blvd. Port-Royal, 5th; Tuesday, Thursday, and Saturday.

Raspail, along the center island of blvd. Raspail between rues du Cherche-Midi and de Rennes, 6th; Tuesday and Friday.

Alibert, rue Alibert and ave. Claude-Vellefaux, 10th; Thursday and Sunday.

Blvd. de Charonne, between rues de Charonne and Alexandre-Dumas, 11th; Wednesday and Saturday.

Pére-Lachaise, blvd. de Menilmontant, between rues des Panoyaux and Tlemcen, 11th; Tuesday and Friday.

Popincourt, blvd. Richard-Lenoir, between rues Oberkampf and Crussol, 11th; Tuesday and Friday.

Richard-Lenoir, blvd. Richard-Lenoir to rue Amelot, 11th; Thursday and Sunday.

Cours de Vincennes, between blvd. Picpus and rue A. Netter, 12th; Wednesday and Saturday.

Poniatowski, odd-numbered side of blvd. Poniatowski, between ave. Daumesnil and rue de Picpus, 12th; Thursday and Sunday.

Gobelins, odd-numbered side of blvd. Auguste-Blanqui, between place d'Italie and rue Barrault, 13th; Tuesday, Friday, and Sunday.

Berthier, corner of ave. de la Porte d'Asnières and blvd. Berthier, 17th; Wednesday and Saturday.

Crimée, 4 to 30 blvd. Ney, 18th; Wednesday and Saturday.,

Lariboisière, side road off blvd. de la Chapelle facing l'hôpital Lariboisière, 18th; Wednesday and Saturday.

Jean-Jaures, 145 to 185 ave. Jean-Jaures, 19th; Tuesday, Thursday, Sunday.

Tolbiac, on two sides of place Jeanne-d'Arc, 13th; Thursday and Sunday.

Alesia, rue d'Alesia, behind the church of St. Anne, 14th; Wednesday and Saturday.

Cervantes, rue Bargue, 15th; Wednesday and Saturday.

Dupleix, blvd. de Grenelle, between rues Lourmel and du Commerce, 15th; Wednesday and Saturday.

What's Cooking?

In Paris you frequently see messages scrawled in what appears to be whitewash on the glass windows of little restaurants and sidewalk *cafés*. The messages describe one or more dishes being offered for lunch and/or dinner inside. And you can be reasonably sure that on that morning the local *marché* sold the restaurant most of the items offered at good or fair prices. These daily bargains usually constitute the restaurant *menu* (fixed-price specials) and *la carte* (bill of fare) specials, as well as the fare served in the homes of nearby Parisians.

These little restaurants are usually Mom-and-Pop operations with one person in the kitchen, one at the cash register, and one who waits

on tables and assists in the kitchen between meals. It is eviden
read the whitewash signs that these establishments offer simple,
known French dishes. Such staples appear as *le bifteck et frites* (th
Parisian favorite), a small, inexpensive, but tasty steak with french
fries; *le pot-au-feu*, the "iron-pot" beef, chicken, and vegetable stew;
les andouillettes, sausage made from the lining of pigs' intestines; *la
blanquette de veau*, rich, creamy veal stew; *le boeuf bourguignon*, dark
tasty beef stew made with red wine; *le petit salé*, ham hock and
lentils; *la daube*, a "back-of-the-stove" beef stew; *le boudin*, blood
sausage usually served with fried apple slices and mashed potatoes; *le
assoulet*, a bean and meat dish baked in a casserole; *la choucroute
garnie*, sauerkraut with ham, bacon, and frankfurters; *le chou farci*,
stuffed cabbage; *le gigot d'agneau*, roast leg of lamb; and *le lapin au
moutarde*, rabbit in mustard sauce. Among the fish offered on these
daily specials are *la barbue*, brill; *le cabillaud*, fresh cod; *le colin*,
whiting or hake; *le merlan*, silver hake; and *le râie*, rayfish.

French food, in spite of what *nouvelle cuisine* chefs and buffs
claim, is not heavy, nor is it necessarily rich. Food in a three-star restaurant, where you are given a demonstration of French culinary
accomplishment, tends to be rich. However, one does not eat in a
three-star restaurant every day, and light, simple dishes are always
available.

Often only one item is posted as the daily special, sometimes,
two, seldom more. And as a rule, only main dishes, not salads, *entreés*
(the appetizer course in France), or desserts, appear. The food is for the
most part prepared in a tiny kitchen occupying minimal space behind
the dining area. Occasionally only one prepared item, the one scrawled
on the window, is offered as an alternative to sandwiches, cheese, or
cold cuts. I have never seen a hamburger offered.

Sandwiches are made from *une baguette* cut lengthwise with a bit
of ham or cheese between the slices. With fresh crisp bread, a quality
cheese or ham (or both), and a touch of sharp Dijon mustard, these
concoctions can be worthy of the French name. The classic hot open
sandwich called *un croque-monsieur* is made with a piece of American-
like bread *(le pain de mie)* with a thin slice of ham and melted cheese.
This formula is not particularly appealing, but there are those who
like them.

Non-French Food

There was a time when one could honestly say, "It's hard to get a
bad meal in Paris." This is no longer true. Hamburger chains, imitation Chinese restaurants run by Vietnamese, Vietnamese restaurants

ers or politicians, cute little Japanese places
beloved by the Japanese, pizza-bakers,
stoned if operating in Naples, and restaurants
, Indians, and Scandinavians have arrived
heap, but many serve food so unwhole-
al. There is no doubt about it, French food
but there is a reason: on the whole it is fresh and
the finest ingredients. Most other cuisines use substitutes
y, cut corners, or use artificial coloring and flavoring and preser-
vatives. The French insist on having proper ingredients and handling
food professionally in both the kitchen and the dining room. Good
French restaurants do not have working college students, only prop-
erly trained personnel, who make a difference in quality as well as
price.

Eating ethnic and other non-French food in Paris, for whatever reason, is a pity. It is true that many French *bistrots* and *cafés* serve medi-
ocre food. Still it tastes better and certainly is more nourishing than
any other food in France.

A History of the Restaurant

Restaurants are not found in the ancient history of Paris. It was a
mere 220 years ago that a caterer with a cooked-food stand defied city
ordinances and the food syndicate laws by serving soup (which was permitted) so thick it became a stew (which was not permitted). It was
the shop of a Monsieur Boulanger, and the year was 1765. He called
his thick soups *restaurants* (restorers), and he was so successful that
the laws were changed to allow solid food as well as soup to be consumed on the premises where it was cooked. Thus the restaurant was
born.

The French, a loquacious race, found eating out much to their lik-
ing, and the restaurant idea spread rapidly. Not only for the convenience and the food, but also as a place for entertainment. The
restaurant became a home away from home; clients had their own
tables, their own napkins, and their "own" waiters or waitresses in
their favorite restaurants. Traces of these traditions remain, creating a
set of unwritten rules that increase the pleasure of eating in France.

At Table With the French

Mealtimes are strictly observed in Paris. Lunch generally is served
from noon to 1:30 p.m., dinner generally from 8 p.m. to 9:30 p.m.
Restaurants are open only for meals (*brasseries, cafés*, and *bistrots*
excepted). Most restaurants do not take orders after 10 p.m.

Restaurants, especially those in the non-tourist neighborhoods, do not all take credit cards. Check before you eat if you are planning to use one.

With rare exceptions (such as student restaurants), tables are never shared with strangers.

Butter, as a rule, is not served with meals, only with certain dishes (for example, sardines and oysters). Almost no restaurants serve soup at midday (the possible exception is *gratinée*, or onion soup, served in *une brasserie*). Coffee is drunk only after dessert, always black and in small cups (not called demitasse—this is an Americanism and unknown in France).

Well-known restaurants listed in guidebooks require reservations in advance. Without a reservation it would not be unusual to be refused and find there are no empty tables available in the neighborhood. Most restaurants do not serve a second sitting. It is important to observe reservations strictly, because even if a little late, a table will be empty and waiting. The New York syndrome of sending patrons with reservations to the bar to wait an hour or more does not exist in France. If you change your plans after making a reservation, phone to cancel. In many simple neighborhood restaurants and, of course, *cafés*, reservations are not necessary.

In restaurants, wait to be seated. Unlike many American eating places, even small restaurants in France expect clients to wait to be seated by whomever is in charge.

Once seated, relax, because no one is going to rush up with a cup of *café au lait*. It takes time. The more elegant restaurants, after a suitable pause and before presenting the bill of fare, may ask if you would like *un apéritif*. In contrast to a cocktail, this usually consists of a concoction only slightly alcoholic. The most popular in France currently is *le kir*. There are several varieties ranging from *un kir royale,* made with a raspberry syrup and champagne, to *un cassis,* the simple original white wine with a trace of red-currant syrup.

When the bill of fare, called *la carte du jour*, is presented you will invariably find *un menu. Un menu* consists of two, three, or more courses for a fixed price.

The price of *un menu* sometimes includes wine and tip, but more often it does not. *(Service et vin compris* means that the cost of the meal includes the cost of tip and wine. *Service et vin non-compris* means they are not included.) *Le menu* is the most economical way to eat in France. It is what the chef has found inexpensive at *le marché.* The portions are smaller on *le menu*, and sometimes *le menu* is only available at specific hours.

In almost all restaurants, a service charge of 15% is included on

73

the bill. It is usual to leave a bit of extra change with your payment, but you need not overdo.

A bit of high school French is enough to handle most *cartes*. A very small pocket-sized book in a washable cover called the *Menu Master for France* or another similar book (usually found on the travel book shelf of almost any English-language bookstore) can be carried for consultation.

If an item appears that has been given a name (usually the first or family name of the chef's mother-in-law) and is obviously not in the *Menu Master*, ask the waiter about it. Waiters in this gastronomic realm have gone to school to learn their trade and know what they serve almost as well as does the chef. Any good waiter will make an effort to explain any dish in great detail (usually making it sound so good it's hard to resist). Many waiters, trained in Swiss or English hotels, have a smattering, if not more, of English. This does not apply, of course, to small neighborhood restaurants where the waiter might be the spouse, son, or cousin of the chef/owner of the establishment. Their training is somewhat less, but the interest and knowledge of food is always enthusiastic.

When everyone has ordered, the wine list is presented. This is separate in more expensive restaurants but either printed along one edge or on the back of *la carte* in less exotic establishments. Again the waiter is usually glad to help make an appropriate choice. In the expensive and highly rated places, *un sommelier*, wine steward, does this expertly. Untrained oenologists should try the house wine, which is usually less expensive and the owner's pride—it is worthy.

The French talk a lot at table and don't appear to have time to eat. But eat they do, usually cleaning their plates in fine consideration of the Armenian food problem. In France it's possible to eat slowly; waiters never rush clients. As a result they can seem slow.

It is difficult to get coffee with dessert, even when the waiter seems to agree to the request. It's best to wait. When the meal is finished, he will bring the coffee as ordered.

The bill will not be presented until asked for, even when clients sit and talk for a half-hour or more after finishing a meal.

The French often drink very strong fruit alcohols (*eau de vie*, cognac, *armagnac*, or *calvados*—applejack) after a meal as a digestive. It is a habit easily acquired, and one that provides much pleasure.

The Great Restaurants of Paris

Michelin publishes a light, easily carried 50-page guide to Paris hotels and restaurants. It is the best guide to restaurants available.

74

Gault and Millau have more up-to-date prices (it's a good idea to add 10% to the *Michelin* prices), but I prefer the *Michelin* choices. I have recommended some restaurants that are in the *Michelin* and a few that are not. In addition, I would like to say a word about the very expensive and highly rated Paris restaurants. An average American coming to France will never really appreciate a $100 to $200 meal any more than a far less expensive one. *Haute cuisine* is for the French or those who live with it constantly. Try to imagine yourself eating a strange dish in Hungary or Japan and wondering what it consists of and if you really like it.

For a really great meal in Paris, the only three-star restaurant I recommend without hesitation is la Tour d'Argent. I also recommend the speciality there, *canard au sang*, duck cooked in its own blood. But anything on *la carte* is good. And you can be fairly sure that if *le maître d'hôtel* feels you are ordering something you aren't familiar with, he will explain it very carefully and recommend gently that you try something else. There are not many restaurants left like la Tour d'Argent. Most of the other three-star Paris restaurants are *nouvelle cuisine* and not at all representative of French food or French cooking.

If you don't have to ask the price, many of the hotel restaurants come up with excellent food—not too many visitors appreciate how good it can be. For super breakfasts or brunches any of the big hotels can be great fun. Le Bristol serves an American-style breakfast for FF80.

Chapter IV

Shopping in Paris

In recent years, a great many of the small Paris merchants—tobacconists, grocers, butchers, bakers, household goods sellers—have disappeared. Many have been replaced by what is referred to as *une boutique* (a retail shop, store, or stand, from the Greek *apotheke*). The goods are sold under a neon glare at markups of some 300% (sometimes called "signature" prices), then reduced during "sales" by a small fraction. But Paris is still a city with wonderful shops.

There are approximately 70,000 shops in Paris—13,000 retail food shops, 40,000 non-food shops, 15,000 wholesale stores, 3 *hypermarchés* (self-service operations with more than 2,500 square meters of floor space), 106 *supermarchés* (more than 400 square meters of floor space but less than 2,500), 12 department stores, and 69 *magasins populaires* (five-and-dime stores). There are also about 300 art galleries in Paris selling paintings, sculpture, and photographs.

La Papeterie

Three splendid shops for paper products are:

Papier +, 9 rue du Pont Louis Philippe, 4th. Closed Sunday and Monday; open noon to 7 p.m. A second shop is located at 86 rue du Bac, 7th. Closed Sunday and Monday morning; open 10 a.m. to 7 p.m.

Mondergueil, 34-36 rue Montergueil, 1st.

At these shops you'll find folders in a terrific array of colors, linen-covered clipboards, and elegant leather binders. These are beautifully displayed, and the owners are usually on hand to welcome you.

Art Supplies

Paris is famous for art supplies. One of the finest shops is **Lavrut**, 52-57 passage Choiseul, 2nd. At this marvelous store you take a number and await your turn. At least 10 knowledgeable salespeople are ready and all set to serve. Le Passage Choiseul is worthwhile even without a visit to Lavrut.

Toys

Jouets et Cie (Toys and Company) is the largest toy shop in France, according to the *Guinness Book of Records*. Stocked with classic toys from all over the world as well as the most modern inventions, this shop is a child's dream. The knowledgeable salespeople can direct you to whatever you have in mind, or you can browse. There is a small select choice of clothing up to size 4 or 6. A T-shirt is available in all sizes with the store's logo—the extraordinary figure of a baby—that squeaks when punched in the stomach. Jouets et Cie has two entrances: 11 blvd. de Sebastopol, 1st; and 16 rue Saint-Denis, 1st, right between le Centre Beaubourg and le Forum des Halles.

Jewelry

One of Paris' most charming women is surely **Jeanne Do**, designer of unusual and delightful jewelry. Her tiny shop is at 67 rue de Seine, 6th, just a short block off le boulevard Saint-Germain. A new collection is designed twice a year, and her use of classic materials is splendid.

Antique Clothes

Anyone interested in antique clothes (most of which are very wearable today), lingerie, or wedding dresses might check the following shops. All three have lovely things.

Les Trois Marchés, 1 rue Guisarde, 6th.
Aux Muses d'Europe, 64 rue de Seine, 6th.
L'Ibis Rouge, 35 blvd. Raspail, 7th.

These stores' hours are a bit vague—best not to try before noon. They are always closed Sunday.

Clothing for Men and Women

Very special sweaters for men and women are found at **Aline Maret,** 12 rue Saint-Sulpice, 6th. These are home-knit, if not always hand-knit, and depending on the season they are in wool, silk, cotton, or combinations of these materials. It's a small shop with very reasonable prices.

Across the street at 3 rue Saint-Sulpice is **Charlotte Munk**, the work place of two charming young Swedish women who design and supervise the making of very simple tailored skirts, trousers, blouses (with matching vests), coats, and wonderful hats.

The local motorcycle crowd buys its leather jackets from **Hein Gericke**, 5 blvd. Richard Lenoir, 11th, just off la place de la Bastille.

Work clothes are bought either at **le Samaritaine** department store, building number 2, 2nd, or **le Didier Delanos**, 67 rue de la Roquette, 11th.

Fashionable French ladies.

The best sweater bargains in Paris are found at **Irlande**, 58 rue Montmartre, 2nd. Scottish cashmeres (brand name Hawica), with crew necks and long sleeves, are FF579 for one-ply, FF865 for two-ply. Aron Isle Irish sweaters are FF449 for pullovers and FF495 for cardigans. All-wool Hawica men's crew neck pullovers are only FF200. This tiny shop has lovely long mohair scarves, FF109 for 60 inches and FF119 for 70 inches. It also carries Kookai knitwear—a French brand very big with young Parisians—at a 20% discount.

Children's Clothing

Wonderful bargains in clothes for young girls (up to size 12), with nothing more than FF100, are at **René Derhy Boutique,** 58 rue Saint-André-des-Arts, 6th. It's a good idea to check the shops next to this one as well. None of the wares are very well-made, but they have lots of charm, and at these prices you can forgive imperfect workmanship.

The trendiest clothes for the very young (up to size 7 or 8) come from **Trotinette**, 54 rue Tiquetonne, 2nd. No bargains, but well-made and irresistible.

Off-price Clothing for Men, Women, and Children

Smart Parisians buy at shops called *solderies*. Some of these sell discounted clothes *with* labels. At others the clothes are *dégriffé*, meaning that the labels have been removed.

The **label-less** shops are found in a row on la rue Saint-Placide, 6th, between la rue du Cherché-Midi and la rue de Sèvres. Shopping there takes patience as you must go through racks and racks and then dig into cartons. For clothes **with labels** (from the last season always), which are much easier to find than the label-less merchandise, try **Cacharel, Hechter, Dorothee Bis,** and others in a row on the odd-numbered side of la rue d'Alesia, 14th, between la rue des Plantes and l'avenue General LeClerc. Also go to **Stock 2,** a Hechter store at 92-94 rue des Plantes. In another category, the **wholesaler Fouks**, 89 rue Réaumur, 2nd (upstairs), has a sale department for women.

Bathroom and Dressing Table Accessories

At 40 rue Saint Sulpice, 6th, you will find **Beauté Divine.** Régine de Robien's boutique has a great selection of period perfume and bath accessories from sponge bowls to towel-drying rods.

Needlepoint/*Merceries*

A great gift for a friend interested in needlepoint is a French needle-point kit. You'll find a good selection at **Laurence Roque,** 69 rue Saint-Martin, 4th, and **l'Atelier d'Anais**, 23 rue Jacob, 6th.

Harder and harder to find in Paris is a good *mercerie,* a shop for buttons, ribbons, zippers, threads, and other sewing supplies. One of the finest is **Maiete Legrand,** 7 Cité Berryer, 8th. This tiny walking street runs from 25 rue Royale to 24 rue Boissy d'Anglais.

Books

America's "minor" publishing houses sell books at the **Village Voice**, 6 rue Princesse, 6th. This bookstore stocks everything current about Paris, except guidebooks. It also has a tea and coffee bar where you can browse and enjoy reading your purchase or a copy of the latest *Village Voice* newspaper. The bar serves a simple luncheon as well.

Special Gifts

Pixi and Company, 95 rue la Seine, 6th, is an extraordinary shop. For the past few years Alexis Poliakoff has been creating and selling wonderful figurines, both *Belle Epoque* and contemporary. You may buy the individual figures, but most are sold in small boxes with a scene painted on the interior so that you can place your personage on stage. The figures are dressed according to trade or period. An artist's studio, for example, has seven subjects with the model lying nude on a sofa. There are Tarzan and Jane swinging in a jungle background, and Stanley on safari looking for Dr. Livingston. Some make splendid souvenirs of Paris, such as a gentleman with *une baguette* under his arm. The box he is sold in says, "Take a Frenchman home with you"— why not? Pixie and Company also sells lead soldiers.

Those who love *la fäience* (earthenware) of **Quimper** will be delighted to find a shop with nothing else at 84 rue Saint-Martin, 4th, just a few steps from le Beaubourg. The shop is simply called Quimper.

A small but very inexpensive gift shop is **l'Arbre á Soldes,** 94 rue de Grenelle, 7th. Nothing too unusual except the prices. They are definitely lower than those for the same objects sold elsewhere.

Museum Shops

Begin with **le Louvre,** where the shops are lined up as a series of boutiques (until the reopening of the "new" Louvre). You'll find the obvious postcards, posters in three sizes, art books, and brochures on various subjects. Prices range from FF4 to FF400. Copies of Egyptian jewelry, key rings designed by today's artists, miniature bronzes, and the remarkable print shops are found on the second floor. This last is open only from 2 p.m. to 5 p.m. and is well worth a visit. Engravings dating back to the seventh century are priced from FF40 to FF400. This is where you can buy the famous 18th-century *plan Turgot* of Paris—20 sheets measuring 20 inches by 32 inches for FF200 each. **La Salle de Chalcographie,** as this boutique is called, is hosted by Madame Gondler. The Louvre items are also sold in **la Boutique** in le Forum des Halles, Porte Bergere, *niveau* (level) 2. This shop carries almost the complete line with the museum logo (including scarves, umbrellas, and tote bags) and is open 10 a.m. to 7 p.m., with the exception of Sunday and Monday morning.

Le Musée des Arts Décoratifs, Pavillon de Marsan, 107 rue de Rivoli, 1st, has been reorganized and now shows its splendid collection of porcelain and period furnishings to great advantage. The ground floor boutique is quite special with gifts of the most modern design as well as porcelain copies of old patterns (*cache-pots* and complete dinner sets). Linens with museum-researched patterns are lovely for either bed or table. There is also an excellent bookshop across the lobby from the gift shop.

Le Musée des Arts de la Mode is next door to le Musée des Arts Décoratifs in the Pavillon Marsan. There you'll find marvelous copies of *l'haute couture* accessories from the late 1940s and 1950s— early Saint-Laurent scarves, Coco Chanel jewelry, and much more.

Across the Seine is the superb new **Musée d'Orsay,** housing works of the Impressionists. The boutique is one of the fine features of this newly organized artistic endeavor. The shop is filled with treasures.

Le Musée d'Art Moderne de la Ville de Paris has an almost undiscovered boutique just inside the entrance. The checkroom on the left sells white cotton tote bags with the museum logo. The straps are long enough to go over your shoulder, and at FF25, the bag is probably the best buy in all Paris. On the right side of the entrance, the gift shop has an amazing collection at reasonable prices. (If staying in Paris any length of time you might join the museum. Annual dues are FF100, FF150 for a couple, FF80 if under 25 or over 60. Members are entitled to reductions of 20% in the gift shop (the FF25 tote becomes FF20!), to meals in the museum cafeteria, *and* to free entry to all other city-run museums.)

Le Centre National d'Art et de Culture Georges Pompidou, commonly known as le Beaubourg, has several splendid boutiques. You'll find the finest selection of postcards and modern art books in Paris and quite a few novelties (stationery, for instance) with the museum's logo.

Although not a museum in the true sense of the word, **la Bibliothèque Nationale** (the French equivalent of the Library of Congress) has a shop in its beautiful, newly redone Galerie Colbert (6 rue des Petits-Champs, 2nd; open Monday through Saturday from 10 a.m. to 6 p.m.). Jigsaw puzzles of historic scenes, compact disks of historic recordings, and lovely stationery with an embossed logo of *la bibliothèque* are sold, all at very reasonable prices.

The Department Stores

Parisians are proud of their department stores, and rightly so. **La**

82

Galerie Lafayette and **Galerie au Printemps,** the two big
Right Bank shops, have true character and style. In these stores you
can find boutiques selling all the internationally known designers,
from Chanel to Kenzo to Louis Vuiton. So if time is limited, do your
shopping in either of these. All the salespeople understand about tax
refunds, and interpreters are available.

The Right Bank has three other department stores. The **BHV** (le
Bazaar de l'Hôtel de Ville) is renowned for its basement hardware department. It sells, for example, 236 varieties of hammers. Then there
is **La Samaritaine,** commonly called La Samar. The top-floor terrace restaurant in *le magasin numéro 2* (store number 2) is worth the
trip just for the spectacular view of Paris. A common Parisian expres-
sion says "you can find everything at La Samar," and it's almost true.

Les Trois Quartiers, located on le boulevard de la Madeleine,
is the most elegant and the least interesting of these stores. It borders
three *arrondissements*, the 1st, 8th, and 9th.

The Left Bank has but one department store: **Au Bon Marché.**
All Left Bank residents tend to shop there at one time or another, and
Madame deGaulle was said to frequent the tea room. Unfortunately,
the tea room has given way to a succession of lesser eating establishments.

On the same floor as the restaurant, you will find antique dealers.
One can always lunch in the department stores. Apart from the
fifth floor cafeteria and restaurant at **La Samaritaine,** in the
summer there is *la Terrasse* on the tenth floor of *le magasin 2.* **La
Galerie Lafayette** has two restaurants on the sixth floor. **Au
Printemps** has *le Grill* on the sixth floor of the "new" *magasin.*
Les Trois Quartiers has *le Quick Lunch* on the fourth floor with a
1930s decor, *le Square* with six boutiques from which to chose your
food, and *la Terrasse* in the summer.

Apart from these department stores, Parisians shop in their local
Prisunic, Uniprix, or **Monoprix.** These are found in every neighborhood, and the styles and even the food products vary according to
locale. They are often good shops in which to buy gifts, lingerie,
sweaters, and almost any daily necessity.

For Collectors

Baskets and boxes: **Les Virtuoses de la Réclame**, 5 rue
Saint-Paul, 4th; 2 p.m. to 7 p.m., closed Monday; **Le Temps
Libre**, 9 rue de Verneuil, 7th; 2:30 p.m. to 7:30 p.m.

Buttons: **La Droguerie**, 9-11 rue du Jour, 1st; **David**, 27 rue
Bonaparte, 6th; **Marguerite Fondeur**, 18 rue d'Anjou, 8th.

Cake and bread molds: **Au Bain Marie**, 20 rue Herold, 1st; **Paeluche**, 2 rue de la Ferronnerie, 1st.

Cameos: **Gillet**, 19 rue d'Arcole, 4th; **Ballan**, Louvre des Antiquaires, Marché aux Bijoux Sous-sol.

Chocolate-candy molds: **Fanfan la Tulipe**, 55 rue du Cherché-Midi, 6th.

19th-century coin purses and boxes: **Abracadabra**, 10 rue de Grenelle, 7th; **Le Coin Reve**, Village Suisse, 78 ave. de Suffren, stands 12 and 15; closed Tuesday and Wednesday.

Combs and barrettes: **Maud Bled**, 20 rue Jacob, 6th; **La Peigne de Venus**, 16 rue du Cherche-Midi, 6th.

Eye glasses: **Musée at Pierre Marly, Optician,** 2 ave. Mozart, 16th; **Chez Colombe**, Marché Paul Bert, alleé 5, stand 198, ave. des Rosiers in St. Ouen; **Brophy**, Marché Biron, stand 135*bis*, ave. des Rosiers in St. Ouen. The latter two are open only Saturday, Sunday, and Monday.

Knives, scissors (all that cuts): **Pierre Bernard**, 1 rue d'Anjou, 8th; **Galerie Marigny**, 2 rue de Miromesnil, 8th.

Opalines: **Abracadabra**, 10 rue de Grenelle, 7th; **Au Petit Hussard**, 5 rue de Beaune, 7th.

Russian "eggs": **A la Vieille Cité**, 350 rue St.-Honoré, 1st; **Natacha**, Cours des Antiquaires, 54 rue du faubourg Saint-Honoré, 8th; **St. Petersburg,** 106 rue de Miromesnil, 8th.

Theater programs: **Bibilor**, 23 rue des Boulangers, 5th; **F. Boutet de Monvel**, 94 rue des Martyrs, 18th.

Trompe l'oeil in porcelain and pottery: **Any Aime**, 25 rue de la Tour, 16th; **Martine Domec**, 40 rue Mazarine, 6th.

Wind-up toys: **Aux Vieux Rats**, 7 rue Pestalozzi, 5th; **Au Petit Mayet**, 1 rue Mayet, 7th.

Wine labels: **A. Combes**, 45 rue de la Roquette, 11th; **Au Coin Musard**, 24 rue Taillandiers, 11th.

Posters: **Artcurial**, 9 ave. Matignon, 8th; **Banque de l'Affiche**, 8 rue de la Cossonnerie, 1st; **Berggruen**, 70 rue de l'Université, 8th; **Claude Bernard**, 5 rue des Beaux Arts, 6th; **Club de l'Affiche**, 49 rue St.-Louis-en-l'Isle, 4th; **A l'Imagerie,** 9 rue Danté, 5th; **Comptoir de l'Image**, 44 rue du Louvre, 1st; **Yvonne Lambert**, 5 rue Grenier-Saint-Lazare, 2nd; **Adrien Maeght**, 42 rue du Bac, 7th; **Maeght-Lelong**, 13 rue Teheran, 8th; **Signature**, 2 Passage Réal, Forum.

Les Passages of Paris

What we call "arcades" are *les passages* to the French, also known as *les galeries*. There is something undeniably intriguing (especially on a rainy day) about wandering through *un passage* with the natural light filtering through a glass roof. Paris' *passages* (from the late 18th and early 19th centuries) were constructed near bus depots, rail stations, theaters, and dance halls to attract customers.

Some still exist today—enough for the visitor to spend a couple hours, or even days, exploring and enjoying the shops and restaurants. Here is a list of the main remaining *galeries*.

Le Passage Bourg-l'Abbé, 120 rue Saint-Denis, 2nd, is an extension of **le Passage Grand-Cerf**. Both are scheduled for restoration in the near future.

Le Passage Brady, 46 rue du faubourg-Saint-Denis, 10th, was opened by a Monsieur Brady in 1828. Though very sad and seedy, it still boasts an excellent art supply shop and an East Indian spice shop.

Le Passage du Prado, 12 rue du faubourg-Saint-Denis,10th, was created in 1785. It now houses a few shops, including a series of "American" shops selling cowboy clothes and boots.

Le Passage du Caire, 239 rue Saint-Denis, 2nd, has three long galleries. It was built on the site of a convent, and the stone paving is partially that of the good sisters' tombs! Originally filled with printers and lithographers, only one remains today. This *passage* is now in the midst of the ready-to-wear district.

Le Passage Choiseul, 36 rue des Petits-Champs, 2nd, is home to le Théâtre Bouffe Parisien. Along its 220 yards are many small shops, an excellent art supply shop (Ledrut, number 52-76), and a wonderful old-fashioned *papeterie* (Boisnard, number 23).

La Galerie Colbert, 6 rue des Petits-Champs, 2nd, magnificently restored, is part of **la Bibliothèque Nationale.**

Le Passage du Havre, 69 rue Caumartin, 9th, consists almost entirely of small shops. There is not much to interest the casual stroller unless he is a model train buff. If so, there is a marvelous shop with miniature trains from all countries and all the bits and pieces that go with model train building.

Le Passage des Panoramas, 10 rue Saint-Marc, 2nd, is the first of three continuing arcades that carry the stroller from la rue St. Marc at the back of la Bourse (stock exchange), across le boulevard Montmartre, and on to la rue du faubourg Montmartre and la rue de Provence. Panoramas has the oldest engraver in Paris: Stern. It has been at number 47 since 1847. Panoramas ends on le boulevard Montmartre, and pedestrians must cross *le boulevard* to continue just opposite to le Passage Jouffroy.

Le Passage Jouffroy, 10 blvd. Montmartre, 9th, offers several restaurants, a wonderful toy shop at number 29 called Pain d'Epice

(Gingerbread), and their extension, a gift shop for adults, at number 35. The second part of *la galerie* has a very good second-hand bookshop called le Velun. *Le musée grévin* (wax museum) is at number 20. At number 46 is l'Hôtel Chopin, a charming, quiet two-star establishment. Le Jouffroy ends at la rue de la Grande Batalière (once a stream that was said to *"porte un bateau,"* or float a boat, after which the street was named).

Le Passage Verdeau is across the street at 6 rue de la Grande-Batelière. The record/guitar shop Vitoz has been at number 1 since 1800; a science fiction bookshop, Roland Buret, is at number 16. Antique records and phonographs are at M. Vitoz Jr., number 26, and a delightful tea/lunch room, la Théière de Jardin, is at number 28. This ends the tour of the three passages that are called collectively les Panoramas.

Le Passage des Princes is at 5 blvd. des Italiens, 2nd. Number 11, l'Ecume de Mer, is the headquarters for Parisian pipe smokers. The shop has been making pipes since 1855.

Le Passage Puteaux, 31 rue de l'Arcade/28 rue Pasquier, 8th, is a very small arcade notable for its pillars and several small boutiques.

The following two *passages* are probably the most interesting, as both have been "revived" while maintaining the atmosphere of the past.

La Galerie Vero-Dodat, 19 rue Jean-Jacques-Rousseau, 1st, was constructed in 1826 by two *charcutiers,* Messieurs Vero and Dodat. It has had the same rules since the period of Charles X: no dogs or parrots allowed. At first opposite a main stagecoach depot, *la galerie* was used by commuters as a shortcut, which brought in a large public. Go to Marie Lecoeur at number 7 for knitwear. The couple at R. & F. Charles at number 14 restores stringed instruments. A very nice restaurant called Clementine is at number 19, and wondrous furniture of the early 1900s can be found at Robert Capia. Great clothes and hats are available at Jean-Charles Brosseau at number 38. It is open daily from 6:30 a.m. to 10 p.m.

La Galerie Vivienne, 4 rue des Petits-Champs, 2nd, connects with le Colbert. For English furniture try Apple Pie, number 29. At Comptoir du Kit, number 42, you can assemble what you need to make jewelry or buy it ready-made. And one of Paris' best places for lunch or tea is A Priori Thé, number 35.

Le Marché aux Puces—Paris' Flea Market

The village of Saint-Ouen is just outside the 18th *arrondissement* beyond the city limits. (Metro end-of-line 4, Port Champerret; bus number 85, Gare de Luxembourg—Saint-Denis.) **Le Marché aux Puces** has been there for nearly 100 years. It is open every Saturday, Sunday, and Monday.

Between 5 a.m. and 7:30 a.m. there are few buyers, but those who show up move fast, checking every item with an experienced eye. Interested only in the items that were not shown the previous week, they buy without hesitation, pay large amounts in cash, and arrange on the spot for shipment to their own warehouses.

From 7:30 a.m. until 7 p.m., *le marché* is open officially for the 200,000 visitors it receives each week. In the 1920s, René Clair described this junk market as "the city of wood and dreams." Today it is better defined as the city of cement and commerce.

Le Marché aux Puces started in 1890 when sanitation laws first required that used clothing and bedding likely to contain vermin not be sold in the city. The rag pickers moved out to a muddy meadow appropriately called "The Plain of the Ill-Seated" that had been used as a military parade ground. They were licensed to sell only to dealers and required to clean all materials before offering them for sale.

A street peddler.

For more than 10 years junk piled up on the muddy plain. Only fanatic collectors and the very poor dared venture into the city of shacks that sprang up.

But when on a cold wet winter's day, a daring buyer spied a genuine medieval tapestry affording a cow protection from the elements, the scene began to change. Word spread, and the market began to attract a large number of regular customers.

In the 1920s, Romain Vernaison, one of the junk dealers, bought a strip of land and built rows of wooden huts that he rented to other dealers. There followed a period when the flea market became fashionable. Le Biron market was built in 1926 and followed by restaurants, bowling alleys, and casinos. Gypsies, tatoo artists, hawkers, fire-eaters, and dancing bear acts filled the alleys between the stands. It became the "in" place for Sunday afternoons.

The carnival atmosphere didn't return in the post-war years, and only one restaurant remained inside the market. The stands were filled with prewar Paris artifacts.

Today there are seven markets in what is now a huge complex. There is less junk, more antiques (both good and fake), and staggering prices.

Le Vernaison, still there, has perhaps the widest variety of bric-a-brac, buttons, frippery, and odd bits of furniture. **Le Biron** has grown chic, with well-waxed (and consequently expensive) antique furniture, art objects, and a bit of jewelry. **Le Paul Bert** has also raised its quality with its prices. There are few traces there of the good old junk, but an interesting selection of spiral stairways. **Le Jules Vallés,** a covered market, has a fine collection of collector's items—toys, post cards, medals, dolls, old newspapers, and magazines. **Le Marché Malik** stocks old clothes and fashionable frippery dresses, hats, leather jackets, and trenchcoats. The newest markets, **le Marché Serpette** and **le Marché Cambo,** specialize in art deco and period furniture, respectively.

Le marché is still a good place to spend a sunny weekend or Monday. You can eat there and at last there is some variety. **Chez Louisette,** in le Vernaison market, allée number 1, was the first postwar restaurant and the only one for many years. **Le Chope des Puces,** 122 rue des Rosiers, opens at 2 p.m. with a sort of Django Reinhardt jazz concert. (Django Reinhardt, a world-famous musician, was a gypsy who played jazz guitar.) A meal can be had for a bit more than FF100 in both these places. The rest offer typical *brasserie/bistrot* food for FF100 to FF150.

A Parisian market.

Chapter V

When You Visit Paris

How much does it cost to visit Paris? That's a difficult question. The logical answer would be that prices depend on fluctuations in the exchange value of the French franc and on the French inflation rate. To some extent they do. But these two factors are far from the whole story.

For example, in 1984, when one U.S. dollar bought 8.74 francs, the cost of a meal at le Restaurant Allard was FF200. The next year, when the dollar bought 8.98 francs, the meal price went down—to FF185. What a great year for an American to eat at Chez Allard! But don't think you would have eaten so inexpensively elsewhere. At la Tour d'Argent, the average cost of a meal went up FF105 during the same period.

And try to explain this, once again using l'Allard as an example. L'Allard had been increasing the price of a meal a moderate three to five francs a year until it lost its distinctive second star in the *Michelin Guide*. Then instead of going down, as one might expect, the price rose FF11.50 the following year.

From 1971 to 1986, the cost of a night at the modest Family Hotel dropped four times, although overall it rose to 3 1/2 times its 1971 rate. And no one seems to know what skyrocketed the cost of a night at the Ritz Hotel—from an expensive $184 in 1985 to an astronomical $402 in 1986!

Hotels

We recommend restaurants in the "Paris by *Arrondissement*" section. Below is a run-down of Paris hotels.

Hotels in Paris, as in the rest of France, are controlled by a government rating system that ranks them from no stars to four. No stars means not recommended; 1 star, minimum amenities; two stars, comfortable; three stars, major tourist hotel and very comfortable; four stars, first-class hotel; and four star *luxe*, a veritable palace of luxury.

Depending on the star rating you can figure that:

89

- no-star hotels cost less than FF150;
- one-star hotels between FF120 and FF220;
- two-star hotels between FF150 and FF300;
- three-star hotels between FF300 and FF450;
- four-star hotels between FF800 and FF1,400;
- four-star *luxe* hotels from FF1,000 and up.

Two New and One Tried and True

The newest hotel in Paris was booked up for its first few months way before the opening date in April 1987. It is ideally located for Left Bank shopping and sightseeing at 9 rue Saint-Benoît, 6th. **L'Hôtel Latitudes** has 110 rooms and is a brand new three-star hotel, not a remodeled one. Prices range from $95 for a single room to $107 for a double in high season (April through October) and from $82 to $95 during the other months. All rooms have televisions and radio alarm clocks, and in *la cave* there is a piano bar. Latitudes is a new chain of hotels and residences located throughout France—in la Côte d'Azur, le Rouret in l'Ardèche, and several ski resorts, most with club atmospheres.

Another comparatively new hotel with an equally splendid address is **l'Hôtel Pavillon de la Reine**. It has four stars and is situated at 28 place des Vosges, 3rd. It is in the heart of le Marais, only a few blocks from the Picasso museum. There are 50 rooms, all with air conditioning and color televisions. Prices are from $115 to $205 for a duplex room for two or three people.

The two-star **l'Hôtel Deux Continents**, 25 rue Jacob, 6th, is on the Left Bank and does not take credit cards. Prices are correspondingly lower, from $35 to $65. The charming owners and staff of this hotel speak English and take excellent care of their clients. The rooms are delightfully decorated.

The Paris Palaces

The more things change, the more they remain the same. Even if they no longer have three servants to each guest—and the guests no longer arrive with their own retinue—the grand palace hotels in Paris still have a lot to offer. As well as comfort and tremendous style, you'll find health clubs, gymnasiums, swimming pools, saunas, workout rooms, heliports, trilingual secretaries, and coiffeurs who offer room service.

In less than a decade, a half-dozen or so Paris palaces have renovated, refurbished, and shifted the character of their services, appealing not only to the wealthy, but to the wealthy business traveler as well.

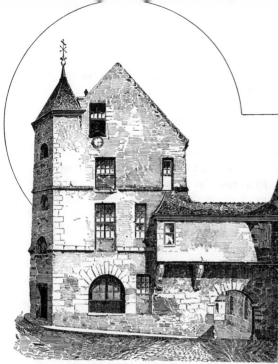

The hotel at 17 rue des Gobelins.

The Taittinger chain put $12 million in l'Hôtel Crillon on la place de la Concorde, creating a palace of marble and gold with the finest materials and furnishings available in the world. In the same period (1981 to 1985), $7 million was spent on le Meurice, more than $14 million on le Prince de Galles, $13 million on le George V, $43 million on le Bristol, $25 million on le Royal Monceau, and $75 million on the Ritz, which was under renovation for six years.

When le Royal Monceau built an exercise center in its basement, the Ritz, not to be outdone, installed a spectacular gymnasium and a cooking school and applied for permission to construct a heliport on the roof. Le Bristol has a new swimming pool rimmed in teak; the shower doors in the rooms are Lalique glass. At le Prince de Galles, the old entrance way has been replaced with a bronze revolving door. Health centers are to be installed at le Plaza Athénée and le George V. The Hilton Suffren has adopted a system of electronic door keys; le Méridien offers 24 television programs (of which 13 are satellite transmissions); l'Intercontinental has a parabolic antenna able to obtain programs directly from the United States.

The trend will continue. Big money is behind the Paris palace circuit: Marriott (le Prince de Galles), Trusthouse Forte (le George V, le Plaza Athénée, la Trémoille), and Grand Met (l'Intercontinental, le Meurice, le Grand Hôtel). A German who is already proprietor of l'Hôtel du Cap at Saint-Jean-Cap-Ferrat and two other hotels in Europe has been offered le Bristol. In 1979 Mohammed al-Fayed (who owns Harrods in London) bought le Ritz for $30 million. The Imperial Suite at the Ritz does not yet have its own sauna, but the price is already up to FF28,980 ($4,800) a night.

One reason for the expensive renovations and room rates is "Americanization"—soundproofing, air conditioning, king-sized beds, suites with jacuzzis, saunas, and solariums. In addition, the hotels need to maintain and magnify their luxury image if they are to retain their wealthy clientele.

But whatever changes, the essential requirement remains personalized service—a quality that began to disappear in the early days of hotel chains. At le Royal Monceau, the receptionist welcomes guests by name right away. The concierge must be ready, willing, and above all able to lease a Boeing jet as easily as to provide a postage stamp.

Further examples of special services offered by *les luxe hôtels* in Paris include:

Golf at la Concorde Lafayette, 3 place de la Porte-des-Ternes. Open Monday to Friday from 7 a.m. to 9 p.m.; Saturday from 9 a.m. to 2 p.m. On the 34th floor you can use a practice green for FF50 a half hour.

Billiards at la Concorde Saint-Lazare, 108 rue Saint-Lazare. Open 11 a.m. to 1 a.m. Play in a room built in 1889 and remodeled by Sonia Rykiel. Six tables, FF36 an hour.

Brunch at the Paris Hilton, 18 ave. de Suffren. Open Sunday from 11:30 a.m. to 2:30 p.m. The menu includes a buffet with fruit juices, salads, delicatessen, poached eggs, pastry, wine, and hot drinks for FF145.

Brunch and Jazz at le Méridien, 81 blvd. Gouvion Saint-Cyr. Open Sunday from noon to 3 p.m. Claude Bolling and his big band (17 musicians) swing while you enjoy a sumptuous buffet, including champagne, pancakes, salads, rollmops, smoked fish, Virginia ham, cheese, and desserts, for FF200.

The Star System: Details

There are 412 **one-star hotels** with a total of 13,744 rooms in Paris. Most measure 86 square feet minimum for one person. Only 20% have private baths or showers and hotel telephones in the rooms.

Hotels rated with **two stars** also guarantee a minimum 86-square-foot room for a single. But 40% have private baths or showers. There is an outside telephone in every room. Buildings four or more stories high have elevators. There are 538 two-star hotels with a total of 20,422 rooms.

Three stars are given to 255 hotels with a total of 12,348 rooms of a minimum 97 square feet for a single. Of these, 80% have a private bath or shower, and all have a telephone with a direct-dial system. There is an elevator in buildings three stories or higher.

Four stars are given to 55 hotels with a total of 6,350 rooms. A single room has a minimum of 107.6 square feet and a bath or shower. There is an elevator in those buildings with two or more floors.

Only 31 Paris hotels are rated **four star** *luxe*. At least 107.6 square feet is guaranteed for a single room, and all have elevators. Rooms have completely equipped bathrooms and direct-dial telephones.

How to Use Paris Post Offices

It is never very far from one of the 163 post offices in Paris, but sometimes the distance to a stamp seems like light-years. In these remarkable institutions are to be found the best examples of French *fonctionnaires* (civil servants). Lines at the windows are unavoidable and the service inevitably poor. I have seen people wait more than an hour at the main post office (52 rue du Louvre, 1st; open 24 hours daily for mail and telephone services) only to discover they were at the wrong *guichet* (window).

With the exception of the one on la rue du Louvre, Paris post offices are open from 8 a.m. to 7 p.m. Monday through Friday and 8 a.m. to 12 noon Saturday. Throughout the city there are 2,200 bright yellow, cheerful-looking mailboxes with pickup times posted on each.

For visitors, *l'aérogramme* (airmail letter), although unexciting, is certainly the most economical choice. It costs FF3.90 with sufficient stamps for any country in the world. The least expensive airmail letter from France to the United States costs FF4.05; a regular-sized airmail postcard costs FF3.35 plus the cost of the card.

The post office sells boxes for shipping goods, but they are fairly heavy. In most cases a padded envelope is more practical and available at any stationery shop (*la papeterie*). Special inexpensive rates for books and printed matter apply when mailing collected guides and maps. Hand-held letter scales are available in most good stationery shops and cost about FF40.

For those planning a long stay in France, the post office will give you a small printout of *les principaux tarifs postaux,* with *le régime interieur et assimilé* on one side and *le régime international* on the other. With this in hand and a scale, it is necessary only to buy stamps. Every post office has a numbered display of all current stamps so that a choice can be made. They are then ordered at *la guichet* marked *les timbres* (stamps), where there is seldom a line.

Regrettably, all advice is useless when it comes to packages. The situation is much too complicated for the space available here. The only information I can give is to advise no package of more than one kilo, or the price immediately becomes astronomical. For more than two kilos you have to go to a central post office. The exception (which proves some very mysterious set of rules) is that up to five kilos of books or other printed matter can be shipped very economically worldwide.

The other useful item available from a post office is *la télécarte*, sold at the stamps window. Almost all public telephones in France now operate with this card, which has replaced the need for a coin. The cards come in two categories: 40 units for FF30.80 or 120 units for FF92.40. This works out to some 0.77 centimes per phone call. Having one in hand is as useful as having a one-franc piece for *une sanisette* (public toilet).

The Public Toilet: a History and Guide

The Roman Emperor Titus Flavius Sabinus Vespasienne (A.D. 9-79), in an attempt to raise the 40-billion sesterces he calculated were needed to balance the state budget, taxed everything, including the use of public urinals. With this act he gave his name to the smelly but architecturally interesting green cast-iron street toilets that dotted Paris streets and *boulevards* for more than 100 years. However objectionable, *les vespasiennes* were an improvement over what had preceded them. For centuries Paris was often described as one gigantic sewer. Everyone threw used water, urine, garbage, and other materials from their windows; in a city of 500,000, infection was rampant.

The first Parisian *vespasiennes* appeared in 1833 sponsored by *le préfet* of the Seine, Comte de Rambuteau. In July 1839 advertising pillars with urinals in the interior were placed along *les grands boulevards*. By April 1843 there were 468 of these maintained by six keepers paid two francs each day. Under the Republic a vast program was launched to increase the number of public toilets. At the height of this trend were *les bornes-fontaines* with candelabras. A veritable battery of models appeared, including the great classic in cast-iron and 820 in other materials. All carried advertising posters on the exterior.

In 1902 a concession was granted for the construction of six kinds of *les chalets de nécessité* open to both sexes and manned by an attendant. In 1911 there were 112 of these in various forms and shapes. By 1930 only 43 were left, and they continued to disappear. A campaign against *les chalets* and *les vespasiennes* waged in the name of public health and sanitation was successful in reducing them over the years. In 1930 there were 1,200; in 1939 only 700; by 1956 the total had dropped to 369; and today there are probably very few left in the entire city. But that is by no means the end of the public toilet in Paris.

94

There are 400 *sanisettes* in the city today, and more are being built. Each costs 100,000 francs to build and is rented to the city for 40,000 francs annually. It is estimated there are 60 users on an average day, 80 to 100 on Sundays. They are not expected to make a profit.

Each *sanisette* consists of a block of white cement ridged on the exterior to discourage the posting of bills and graffiti. The interior, lit by natural and artificial light, is heated, wired for muzak, and expertly ventilated. For a one-franc coin the user is allowed in, can lock the door, and has a choice of sit-down toilet (*á l'Anglaise*) or a squat (*á la Turque*). There's a wash basin, perfumed toilet paper, and hooks for hanging clothing and handbags. In the event of an emergency (should someone faint or need help), a siren sounds automatically if the cabin is not vacated in 20 minutes.

When the user leaves, the door rolls closed automatically. During a cycle of 45 seconds the toilet swings against the wall into a very fast twirling brush and is simultaneously sprayed with a perfumed disinfectant. Once brushed and sprayed it is dried by a current of hot air and ready for the next customer.

The Best Restaurant Toilets (and Telephone Facilities)

The best toilets in Paris are at la Brasserie Bofinger and le Café Costes, with Chez Français a close runner-up. **Bofinger,** 3-7 rue de la Bastille, 4th, offers art deco style as well as comfort. You'll find beautiful tile work, brass faucets, and generous double sinks mounted on an antique cabinet. On the wall, framed in blue tile, a topless figure tells an allegorical story. A light lavender odor prevails. A telephone, well apart, is in a roomy booth.

Close on the heels of Bofinger is **le Café Costes** (the one at place des Innocents, 1st). Quite different from Bofinger, this toilet is like *le café* above it—starkly simple, with glass and mirrors everywhere. There are no faucets and no soap; hands are washed in running water turned on by a foot pedal.

At **Chez Français,** 7 place d'Alma, 8th, the toilets are found at the foot of a magnificent rose marble staircase. Fresh flowers, isolated telephones in glass cabins, built-in sinks, and mirrors afford lots of taste and style.

Less glamorous but with old-fashioned chic are the facilities of **les Deux Magots**, 170 blvd. Saint-Germain, 6th. A single wash basin (a beautiful antique) serves for both men and women. The telephone, controlled by an attendant, is limited to three-minute conversations.

The toilet at **la Fortune des Mers,** 53 ave. d'Italie, 13th, does it up in good modern taste, with a delightful blue telephone living in an alcove quite apart from the cloak room and the restaurant.

Le Sauvignon, a wine and sandwich bar run for the past 30 years or so by the Vergne family at 80 rue Saints-Pères, 6th, deserves honorable mention. Described by an expert as *"sportif,"* the toilet is found at the top of what easily might be the steepest scrubbed wooden stairway in Paris. The W.C. is a historic model (*á la Turque*—said to be much healthier for those with digestive problems). The sink is very small. A heavy cotton hand towel adds a touch of class.

One of the busiest in town is the combined coat room, telephone room, message center, and toilet at **la Coupole,** 102 blvd. du Montparnasse, 14th. With a little decoration this could rival the facilities at les Deux Magots or la Fortune des Mers. At present it is painted a depressing gray. Automatic soap and towel dispensers add no charm, although the Western-style swinging doors that separate the toilets from the telephone and hat check counter provide a touch of glamor. La Coupole is a good place to receive a telephone call; staff members circle around the two acres of tables with a blackboard bearing your name (inevitably misspelled). There is also a place to leave or receive letters—a nice touch but suspect, as the same letter has been on the board for the past 20 years.

There are a half-dozen wine bars around town, including **l'Ecluse** (we're speaking of the one located at la rue Mondetour in the les Halles neighborhood, 1st). There's a clean if stark toilet and telephone down a chocolate-colored hallway. Nice touches of security—a protection, one supposes, for those who might have sampled too much of the splendid wines available here.

Reading a Map of Paris

When using a map of Paris, first figure out the direction you are taking in relation to the Seine. House numbers run up in the direction of the river's flow—lower numbers upstream, higher numbers downstream. Streets that run perpendicular to the river are numbered from the river—lower numbers are near the river, higher numbers are farther away.

This ingenious system works about 80% of the time, but one must beware of the exceptions. The great 19th-century rebuilder of Paris, Haussmann, and his successors sliced through and across thoroughfares at various angles with utter abandon. When rebuilding on these newly created streets, they often had to construct prow-shaped or flatiron buildings. In addition, many streets have similar names.

Paris street names have originated from places (for example, rue du Bourg-l'Abbé, rue du Clos-Bruneau), someone famous (rue Simon-le-France, rue d'Aubry-le-Boucher), a nearby building (rue Saint-Germain l'Auxerrois, rue du Temple), a collection of artisans (rue de la Ferronnerie—ironworkers, rue de la Verrerie—glassworkers), and in earlier days very often from a sign (rue de l'Arbre-Sec, rue de la Huchette).

The original names were often mutated by the population using them—*la rue Salalie* became *la rue Zacharie; la rue Thibaut-aux-Des* became *la rue Thibautodé*; and *la rue Jeux-Neuf* became *la rue Des Jeuneurs*.

Beginning in the 17th century, many streets were named after the royal family (Louis-le-Grand, Thérèse) or famous ministers (Richelieu, Colbert, Mazarine). Later, names of the more lowly were included, such as civil servants, merchants, and writers (Michodière, Caumartin, Taitbout), and even later, names of the revered dead (Corneille, Racine).

During the Revolution, the names of grand ideas and great men of the epoch replaced most of the street names that referred to nobility. Later, when Napoléon and Haussmann created many new streets, they named them for victories and famous men from history as well as members of the imperial family (Magenta, Turbigo, Copernic, Impératrice, Roi-de-Rome).

In early Paris there were no signs to indicate the names of streets, nor were there maps. It often took hours to find a destination. In the early 18th century, an ordinance decreed that a canvas name plaque with black letters on a yellow background be placed on the first and last building of each street. These proved too fragile, and the regulation was changed from the plaque to a stone embedded in the wall of a house with the street name and quarter engraved on it. These are still found throughout Paris.

The stone indicators were replaced in 1823 with metal plaques painted black with white characters placed at one end only of each street. These were replaced in 1844 with the familiar enamel plaques with white letters on a blue background.

The 1860 annexations of suburban localities caused a lot of confusion, because many street names already existed in Paris and other villages. Each new quarter had to find new names for a great many streets.

An abortive attempt to replace house signs with numbers for identification began in 1507. Other attempts were equally unsuccessful, and it was not until 1775 that numbers were painted on the houses inside the city walls in numerical order. The system went up one side of the street and, including courts, cul-de-sacs, and alleys that opened onto the street, back down the other side. Using this system, the house across from number 2 rue Garancière, a street about 700 feet long, became number 1096.

This system did not work. In addition to its impracticality, the owners of grand mansions resented being numbered along with cobbler's booths. And everyone saw it as a potential means of determining a new tax.

A new numbering system was put into use during the Revolution. It was determined by administrative sections and limited to them. Streets that ran through several sections had houses with similar numbers, which caused much confusion. The present day numeration was instituted in 1805.

The Best Way to Tote Your Stuff

Purse snatchers are a force to be reckoned with in Paris, as in most European cities. A shoulder bag should be used to carry only necessities. Put hard-to-replace essentials, such as **passports**, **travelers checks**, and **credit cards,** in a buttoned pocket or shirt.

A 10-inch-by-15-inch shoulder bag with a half-dozen compartments, some large, some small, provides the handiest means of toting all the necessary paraphernalia for comfortable traveling. Below is a list of items you might find useful while making your way through Paris.

Small memo pad for notes.

Small telephone/address book with European names/numbers.

International driver's permit.

SNCF (railroad) *carte de couple/famille.*

SNCF calendar (showing given days one may travel with reduced-fare tickets).

Xerox copy of a list of names, addresses, and telephone numbers of European auto clubs affiliated with AAA.

Timetables.

#5 Opinel knife.

Tekna-Lite flashlight.

Corkscrew.

Box of Sucrettes.

One resealable storage bag.

Two large keys to your hotel, apartment, or house.

Ball point pen.

Automatic pencil.

Small comb.

Small resealable plastic bag with disposable moist towelettes, band aids, safety pins, aspirin, and antiseptic cream.
Six-inch plastic rule (metric/linear).
Slide rule pocket metric converter.
Box of wooden matches.
Folding pocket magnifying glass.
Berlitz *French for Travelers*.
Detailed *plan* (map) of Paris by *arrondissements*.
Small French/English dictionary.
Small tourist office map of Paris.
Clipping of current exhibitions in Paris.
Plan of le Musée National d'Art Moderne (Beaubourg).
Notes on exhibits, etc. (prepared prior to departure).
Packet of paper tissues.

The Louvre.

Chapter VI

Filling Your Paris Days

Pariscope and *l'Officiel des Spectacles*, weekly pocket-sized magazines, list all current attractions in Paris. You can buy copies at newsstands all over the city. Paris has more than 60 theaters, most on the Right Bank. (There is no equivalent to New York's Broadway.) In addition, there are 32 cafe-theaters, 95 cabarets with dancing, 22 music halls, 2 permanent circuses, 10 orchestras, 48 concert halls, and 15 jazz concert halls. There are another 10 very active suburban theater groups. And there is l'Opéra, l'Opéra Comique, le Théâtre Musicale de Paris (T.M.P), le Théâtre de Paris, le Théâtre des Champs-Elysées, and la Salle Gaveau and la Salle Pleyel, which serve as opera, ballet, and concert halls. The choice is large.

Entrance to le théâtre des Varettes.

A booth called le Théâtre Kiosque (15 place de la Madeleine, 8th) is open from 12:30 p.m. to 8 p.m. (it closes at 6 p.m. on Sunday). Here you can obtain theater tickets for that same day at half price.

Paris nights start late. Here are a few places to dance:

La Scala, 188*bis* rue de Rivoli, 1st; tel. 42.61.64.00. FF80 entry includes one drink; refills are FF45 to FF50. Ladies enter free except Friday, Saturday, and holiday evenings. Open 10 p.m. to dawn.

Le Slow Club, 130 rue de Rivoli, 1st; tel. 42.33.84.30. FF45 entry on week nights; FF60 on Friday and Saturday. Refills are FF10 to FF60. Live jazz. Closed Sunday and Monday.

Le Balajo, 9 rue de Lappe, 11th; tel. 47.00.07.87. FF70 entry at night; afternoons from 3 p.m. to 6:30 p.m., FF30 to FF35. Open Friday, Saturday, and Monday evenings from 10 p.m. to 4 a.m. A bit of everything and everyone. 50 years old and still going strong.

La Chapelle des Lombards, 19 rue de Lappe, 11th; tel. 43.57.24.24. African and reggae. Prices vary according to the group playing. Open from 10:30 p.m. to dawn.

La Main Jaune Square de l'Amerique Latin, Porte de Champerret, 17th; tel. 47.63.26.47. Dancing with or without roller skates. Prices vary according to the day and hour. Closed Sunday, Monday, and Tuesday. Open 3 p.m. to 7:30 p.m. and 10 p.m. to dawn.

Utopia Jazz Club, 1 rue Niece, 14th; tel. 43.22.79.26. Small groups. Bluegrass every other Tuesday. Closed Sunday and Monday.

Piano Bars are for listening and drinking, usually not for dancing. Seldom is there a piano player.

See also **Montmartre** in the section on the 18th *arrondissement*.

Learning the Language

Paris offers many different schools. For small classes and individual attention when **learning French,** try a school called *l'Etoile,* 4 place Saint-Germain-des-Près, 6th; tel. 45.48.00.05.

If you want to work on your accent or on a specific subject in French, an excellent professor for **private French lessons** is **Catherine.** She can be reached at tel. 43.73.58.45.

One of the nicest ways to learn French is in **cooking classes.** In the kitchen of Claudine Loez, groups of not more than six people meet regularly, prepare the meals, and eat them. Claudine, who is bilingual, does the shopping, but the pupils do all the rest under her supervision. Not only do you learn a great deal about French cooking, but you acquire a bilingual approach to food and make friends at the same time. Special classes can be arranged for *la pâtisserie* (pastry making) or whatever you wish. This young woman spends the month of August teaching in the United States but is available the rest of the year at 10 rue des Quatrefages, 5th; tel. 45.35.32.88.

And once you speak French and have learned to cook, you can try the **lace-making school** and museum, *l'Atelier de la Dentellière,* located at 9 rue Patay, 13th.

Being Buried

The first major Paris cemeteries, created during the Roman Occu pation, were outside the city walls. Roman sanitary laws required that bodies be buried well away from inhabited areas. Eventually, as the city grew and the new walls included the older cemeteries, the law was disregarded.

By the 6th century, privileged people were authorized to bury their dead near their churches, usually within the city walls. In addition, chapels and other religious establishments (abbeys, priories, convents, colleges, seminaries, and hospitals) maintained their own burial grounds on the premises. This situation, entirely contrary to good public health practice, continued until 1775. Bodies of ordinary people were interred in communal graves that remained open until a layer of bodies was achieved. This often resulted in pestilence and unpleasant odors throughout the neighborhood of the church or abbey.

When, in 1780, the wall in the cellar of a food market in les Halles collapsed and discharged dozens of bodies into the same cham ber as stacks of food, the rules were rewritten and cemeteries were once again moved outside the walls. The exceptions were Père-Lachaise in the eastern part of the city, Montmartre in the north, and Montpar nasse in the south.

In 1880 Paris once again expanded beyond its walls to include many villages and communities that surrounded the city. Eleven ceme teries were included in the annexation.

Before the French Revolution, 9 abbeys or priories, 108 convents for men and women, 69 churches, 31 chapels, 30 hospitals, 10 col leges, and 12 seminaries in Paris maintained cemeteries. In the 1780s, the catacombs (underground quarries dating from Roman times) were converted to a vast charnel house. The bones that lay under Parisian soil were taken there for permanent storage.

The Museums of Paris

The *Michelin Green Guide* gives a list of the museums of Paris by subject. Our list includes only new museums or those undergoing changes.

There are three major new museums in Paris. **Le Picasso** opened in the summer of 1986. **Le Musée de Science, Technologie, et Industrie** at la Villette opened in the spring of 1986. And **le Musée d'Orsay** opened in December 1986.

Le Musée de Science has scientific exhibits for children and adults that can be touched, manipulated, and experimented with and

103

ons. It is perhaps one of the most modern techno-
e world.

it is located, is a complex of cultural, educa-
ities built on 136 acres of land that was once a
house located on the very edge of northwest

.s a village" of activity, with the museum, a the-
ater, a music hall, an exhibit hall (formerly a huge stock shed), a
spherical screening room *(Geode)*, and a "music city" or conservatory.
All are in a public park constructed around the junction of two canals.

The **Picasso museum** is the result of a 1968 law that permits
heirs to pay inheritance taxes with works of art instead of money.
This was an obvious solution for the Picasso estate.

What is especially fascinating about this museum is that it contains an intelligent selection of all the artist's life work. The collection charts the fascinating course of Picasso's artistic development
through the rooms of a magnificent 17th-century mansion.

Located beside the Seine across from the Louvre, **le Musée
d'Orsay** is in a former railway station and luxury hotel. Built in
1900, abandoned in 1939, and saved from demolition in 1971, this
converted rail station houses the art of the second half of the 19th
century and the early years of the 20th.

Le Musée d'Orsay has inherited the collections of le Jeu de Paume
museum, elements from the modern art collection of the city of Paris
(le Palais de Tokyo), appropriate works from the Louvre, and art from
regional French museums. The collection has also grown through
donations, works acquired in payment of inheritance taxes, and paintings purchased since le Musée d'Orsay's inception in 1978. The entire
collection consists of 2,300 paintings and 250 pastels, 1,500 sculptures, 1,100 art objects, and 13,000 photographs, as well as sketches,
plans, drafts, models, and mock-ups.

The building has an elegant restaurant, as well as a separate lunchroom.

Le Centre Georges Pompidou is now the number one Paris
attraction, with 25,000 visitors a day. (That's twice as many as la
Tour Eiffel and almost equal to Disneyland.) The building, high-tech
in the extreme, is an attraction in itself. The permanent collection,
recently reorganized by Gae Aulenti (who designed the installation of
le Musée d'Orsay), is one of the finest of modern art. It includes works
by Picasso, Braque, Chagall, Leger, Brancusi, Dali, and many other
important artists. But only 20 out of 100 visitors to the center spend
time in the collection. Of the rest, 50 go directly to the library, 20 to
the various temporary exhibits, and 10 simply stroll around.

104

The 400,000-volume library averages 11,000 visitors a day and up to 19,000 a day on weekends. Unfortunately, only 2,000 people are admitted at a time. Lessons in 95 different languages are available, with a choice of more than 400 learning systems.

Le Louvre, started in the 12th century as a palace for the kings of France, has been a museum since the 18th century. It is now under extensive reconstruction. When finished, le Louvre will not only be the largest museum in the world, but also one of the most fascinating to visit. A controversial glass pyramid (three

The Tuileries.

stories high) will cover a new underground entrance in the main court that faces le Jardin des Tuileries. Parking arrangements, shops, *cafés* and restaurants are being added underground.

Jobs in France

Any registered full-time matriculating student (undergraduate or graduate) who is a U.S. citizen or a permanent resident of the United States may work in France for three months at any time of the year. Anyone interested in this program should contact Work Abroad, Council on International Educational Exchange, 205 E. 42nd St., New York, NY 10017. This program enables students to earn while they learn and to obtain a fresh point of view that could never be realized while vacationing. The application fee of $82 covers the paper work necessary to assure the legality of your work status for the three-month period. No one without proper work papers is entitled to work in France.

In the Swim

Paris summers sometimes get hot and sticky, but for relief from such weather there are plenty of swimming pools located in every quarter of town. During the summer months the 24 public pools are open from 2 p.m. to 7:30 p.m. Tuesday through Saturday and from 8 a.m. to 6 p.m. Sunday. On certain days of the week each pool stays open until 8 p.m. The most convenient and pleasant, la Piscine Deligny, is privately owned. La Deligny is an uncovered pool floating on the Seine just across the river from la place de la Concorde (Quai Anatole-France). It is open daily from 9 a.m. to 7 p.m. Topless clients add to the charm.

The American Library in Paris

The American Library in Paris is the oldest and largest English-language library in Europe, with more than 100,000 books and a collection of 350 periodicals. In 1928, Stephen Vincent Benet wrote *John Brown's Body* in the reading room. The library was also used by Gertrude Stein, Louis Bromfield, and Thornton Wilder. It has been an arena for debates by such formidable figures as John Kenneth Galbraith, Raymond Aaron, and Charles Frankel. It survived and grew through the Great Depression, the Occupation during World War II, the Liberation of Paris in 1944, the street riots of 1968, and the energy crises of the mid-1970s.

During the past five years, the American Library has been having a resurgence, developing a program that the trustees believe will be more responsive to the needs of the international community in Paris. Aging and fragile periodicals are being replaced by microfilm, and certain operations are being computerized.

To continue this expansion, the library must raise $50,000 a year. Anyone wishing to contribute may send a donation to The American Library in Paris, 10 rue General Camou, 75007 Paris.

Chapter VII

Getting Around Paris

Riding the buses is more expensive than taking the metro if you are using tickets. On the metro one single ticket will take you anywhere in the city with as many transfers as you wish. On the other hand, you have to use a second ticket on a bus if you go beyond two sections of the city, and if you transfer from one bus to another it costs an additional ticket each time.

It is more economical and convenient to purchase a daily, weekly, or monthly bus pass to use during your stay in Paris. The

Le boulevard Montmartre.

passes are valid for both the metro and buses. On the metro you use your little ticket like a token; on a bus you simply show the pass to the driver as you get on.

In December 1986 a single ticket cost FF4.50 when purchased separately (you can buy one from the bus driver as you get on), and FF2.75 when purchased in *un carnet* of 10 (*carnets* are available in any metro station).

Une carte orange is a daily, weekly, monthly, or annual pass to all buses, the metro, and the RER (*Réseau Express Régional,* or Regional Express System), when used inside the city limits.

107

A second-class one-day *carte orange* can be bought for FF19. You'll pay FF43 for a second-class one-week pass, FF152 for a monthly pass, and FF1,600 for a year's "free" rides.

The Paris metro system has:

- 46 miles of corridors
- 37 miles of station platforms
- 315 stations *intra-muros*, 365 total
- 123 miles of track plus 60 miles of RER
- A longest line of 14 miles (Balard-Créteil)
- 21 elevators in 10 stations
- 387 escalators
- 600 trains circulating simultaneously
- 300 station stops
- 138-million passengers annually on the busiest line, Porte d'Orléans-Porte de Clignancourt
- 35-million people a year who use the busiest station, Saint-Lazare (the least-used station is Eglise d'Auteuil)

Paris metro trains do not travel as fast as those in New York City, but they are much more frequent all day long. Nor do they travel as far as those in New York.

The RER

The RER (the new suburban trains) goes north, south, east, and west to suburbs outside Paris. Consult the maps for use. You can ride the trains inside the city limits with your metro ticket, but to go to the suburbs you will have to buy a special ticket. The RER tickets are very sophisticated. To get onto the platform you must run yours through a turnstile that marks the ticket magnetically indicating the station where it was used, then returns it. Keep your ticket, you will need it to leave the station at the other end of your ride. If the turnstile opens and keeps your ticket as you leave, you have paid the correct fare. If it does not open and a buzzing noise sounds, you owe more money for your ride and must go to the window and settle up.

Life in the Underground

There is a lot going on in the clean and well-heated Paris subway. There are photo labs, fruit stands, candy vendors, florists, and in one station, even a vending machine for blue jeans. A shop called Chic Choc at the station Châtelet-Les Halles sells souvenirs related to the metro.

Some of the stations are elaborately decorated with permanent displays, usually relating to the history or activity of the neighborhood above. L'Hôtel de Ville stop has a marvelously informative exhibit of the history of the seal of Paris and of la place de Grève, the square in front of l'Hôtel de Ville. The Saint-Germain-des-Près station has a detailed picture history of the neighborhood on one platform and of printing on the other. (The area is the book publishing section of town.) A station called Parmentier on the Levallois-Gallieni line has a theme of potatoes, because a man named Parmentier introduced potatoes to France. The stations Victor Hugo, Pasteur, and Javel-André Citroen each have appropriate decorations. And an abandoned station, Croix Rouge, has a colorful beach scene along the entire length of the unused platform. Figures in bathing suits bask in the glaring light.

Special events are scheduled in certain stations year-round. You'll find concerts, photo exhibits, dance groups, theater, even a boxing match. Some stations are equipped with video screens showing advertising clips. And there are dozens of "underground musicians"— students of music who practice in the metro to supplement their income—as well as country and rock groups who usually play and sing American music.

The City Bus System

The Paris bus network is a classically thought-out transportation system. The routes of each of the 55 bus lines have changed very little since World War II. When used for sightseeing in the city, 17 of these lines are excellent, and we will describe them anon. With *une carte orange* you can ride from end to end as often as you wish for no additional cost.

There are 54 numbered bus lines plus *la Petite Ceinture (P.C.,* little belt line) that runs in both directions from port to port around the outer edge of Paris. In addition, the mini special Montmartrobus saves one from the exertion of climbing the steepest hill in Paris, Montmartre.

To use the numbered buses you must first determine, on a map or otherwise, the direction of your destination from where you are. You then check a map for a bus that goes from your point of origin to your destination. (City bus maps are found on the back of covered bus stops or given free at metro ticket windows. And a bus map and a route indicator or chart are available for all lines.) Look at the end of the line for the terminals. On buses, terminals are displayed above the windshield. Terminal signs are changed at each end to indicate in which direction the bus is traveling.

It is good to know these few general facts about the system as well:

1. All buses with numbers in the 20s originate or terminate

(according to the direction) at la Gare Saint-Lazare; all those numbered in the 30s at la Gare de l'Est; those in the 40s at la Gare du Nord; and those in the 90s at la Gare Montparnasse.

2. At each stop there is a map/chart of stations that indicates the direction the bus will take. Only buses that use the stop will be posted.

3. Every bus stop provides such information as:
   a. The times the first and the last buses pass.
   b. The frequency of the buses at various times of the day and on different days of the week.
   c. The days buses do not operate.
   d. The nearest night bus stop.

From the disks on the yellow and red bus stop signs you can tell the number of buses that stop there. If the number is black in a white circle, the bus runs on Sundays and holidays (and usually later than the others that do not); if the number is white in a black circle, the bus does not run on Sundays and holidays (*sauf dimanche et fêtes*).

4. At night, 13 regular bus lines and *la P.C.* operate until midnight or 12:30 a.m. They are not always the same lines as those that operate on Sundays, and they do not make full (terminal-to-terminal) runs after 8:30 p.m.

Using the Paris buses is a pleasant way to get around town. The metro is simpler and perhaps easier to use at first, but one misses so much of the city while underground. Buses are convenient, too. Almost no locations in the city limits are farther than a few blocks from a bus. And buses run to all the nearby suburbs, to Rungis (the central food market), and to both airports.

Paris by Bike

During the past three years, paths have been created for cyclists in various parts of the city. They are short and not connected with each other. Most follow along the canals or unused railroad beds. Present plans call for a total of one-and-a-half miles of cycle path in Paris—not much when compared to the 230 miles reserved for automobiles.

To rent a bicycle, here are three addresses:
Paris Velo, 2 rue du Fer-a-Moulin, 5th.
PGL, 40 rue Gay-Lussac, 5th.
Bicy-Club de France, 8 Porte Champerret, 17th.

Cabbing It

The cab tariff per kilometer (0.6 mile) is FF2.39 *intra-muros*.
Between 6:30 a.m. and 9 p.m. in the suburbs of Seine-St. Denis,
Hautes-de-Seine, and Val-de-Marne, the cost is FF3.72 per kilometer.
The fixed pre-mileage reading is FF8. The fees for airports and railway
stations are FF3.80. Waiting-time charges are FF65 an hour. Baggage
supplement is FF2.50, and "bulky packages" cost from FF3 to
FF3.20.

If the light on the roof of a taxi is fully lit, the taxi is available,
except when the driver is on his way home and will not take anyone
who is not going his direction. As a general rule, taxis will not pick
you up if you are not within 100 meters (about 100 yards) of a taxi
stand. These are clearly marked with blue and white metal signs on
corners throughout the city. There are a number of "telephone" taxi
companies; bear in mind that these start the meter as soon as they
receive the order with your address. In most cases, it is considerably
less expensive to find a taxi nearby. But telephoning is obviously
practical when burdened with luggage and headed for an airport, or if
one must make a very early or very late rendez-vous with little chance
of finding a taxi.

SITU—the Automatic Transit Consultant

SITU (*Système d'Information sur les Trajets Urbains*, or Urban
Transportation Information System) is a very intelligent computer
that has memorized 100,000 Paris street addresses. The nine experimental boxes are installed in key positions around Paris. You type in
a question, such as, "How do I get to such-and-such an address fast-
est?" You also can specify that you want the route with the shortest
walking distance or whether you are traveling by metro or bus.

Sightseeing in Paris on City Buses

The best bus lines for sightseeing purposes are 24, 29, 30, 32,
38, 42, 47, 52, 58, 63, 69, 72, 73, 75, 82, 84, and 87. Use buses for
sightseeing during the off-hours after 10 a.m. and before 5:30 p.m. In
summer, when it remains light until later, from after 7:30 p.m. until
the bus stops running is equally acceptable.

111

Remember, with your *carte orange* you can get off the bus, visit a museum, walk through a neighborhood, have lunch or coffee, then get back on and finish your tour without paying any additional charges.

For information on both the bus and metro systems, ask at the metro ticket windows.

Nine Scenic Bus Routes

These scenic itineraries should be accompanied by the *Michelin Green Guide to Paris*. In our opinion, it's the best historical and architectural guide to Paris. Where we think the *Michelin* should be read, we have noted the relevant page number and *MGG* in parentheses.

1. Bus 24: Gare Saint-Lazare to Alfort

Operates weekdays from 7 a.m. to 8:30 p.m.; no service Sunday or holidays. Average wait between buses: 8 to 13 minutes weekdays; 12 to 15 minutes Saturday.

La Gare Saint-Lazare is the site of Monet's railroad station paintings. Compare the station with one of the paintings in le Musée d'Orsay. The steam trains are gone, but the superstructure of the station is quite the same.

La Gare Saint-Lazare was the first Paris train station. Built in 1873, it was originally a few blocks south behind la Madeleine. Later, the station was moved to la rue d'Amsterdam and la rue Saint-Lazare (from which it took its name). It was enlarged in 1885 and then modernized in 1930.

The 24 bus takes la rue Tronchet to the back of **la Madeleine**, the church of Saint Mary Magdelen, and goes around it affording good views on three sides. (For a well-told account of the stormy life of this famous landmark, *see p. 61, MGG*.)

Notice the elegant shops and the famous restaurant Maxim's on **la rue Royale**. There the bus crosses **la rue St. Honoré**, the Fifth Avenue of Paris.

Entering **la place de la Concorde** is always a thrill. It's the largest square in Paris and one of the most beautiful in Europe. It is also one of the most historic—Louis XIII was guillotined here in 1793 *(p. 43, MGG)*.

Across la place de la Concorde and over the bridge is **le Palais Bourbon**, which has been refaced with pillars to match those of la Madeleine on the other side of the Seine. As it approaches the bridge over the Seine, the bus turns left onto the riverside drive that skirts **le Jardin des Tuileries** *(p. 40, MGG)*.

112

Across the Seine, the 87-year-old train station **la Gare d'Orsay** is now a museum of late 18th- and early 19th-century art and artifacts. When this magnificent station was built, a visitor remarked that it looked like les Beaux Arts and les Beaux Arts looked like a railroad station. "They should switch before it's too late," he quipped.

As **le Louvre** comes up on the left, the bus passes (on the right) **le Pont Royal**. Built in 1865, it replaced a footbridge painted red (le Pont Rouge) that had replaced the Tuileries ferry established in 1550. (La rue du Bac, on the other side of the bridge, got its name from the French word for ferry.)

The next bridge, **le Pont du Carrousel**, is opposite le Louvre arches that lead to the arch of the Carrousel and **le Cours Napoléon**, where a three-story-high glass pyramid is being built to cover the new entrance to le Grand Louvre.

As the bus continues along the south side of le Louvre—the largest building in Paris—a footbridge on the right leads across the river to **le Palais de l'Institut**, the home of **l'Académie Française** *(p. 138, MGG)*. This bridge, recently reconstructed, is called le Pont des Arts, probably because its view of le Pont Neuf and l'Ile de la Cité has long been a popular subject for professional as well as Sunday painters, who line the bridge in good weather *(p. 138, MGG)*.

The bus turns right onto the next bridge, **le Pont Neuf.** Though the name means *new bridge*, le Pont Neuf is the oldest in Paris. To the right of the bus, as it reaches the halfway point on l'Ile de la Cité, there stands a splendid statue of good King Henri IV, who laid the cornerstone in 1578. He faces the charming little place Dauphine, also his creation *(p. 62, MGG)*.

Bus 24 does not cross the river but turns left on **le Quai des Orfèvres** (goldsmiths). In the 17th and 18th centuries, *le quai* was the Paris jewelry center. Today **le Palais de Justice** (law courts) is located there.

After passing le boulevard du Palais (left) and le Pont St. Michel (right), the bus arrives at the corner of the parvis of Notre Dame.

As the bus turns right on **le Petit Pont**, look left for a good view of Notre Dame. Le Petit Pont, built in 1853, spans the river at the exact site of a wooden bridge built by the Romans.

Then on the Left Bank and la rue Saint-Jacques (the Roman road to Orléans), the bus passes behind the Gothic church of Saint-Sèverin. The story of this church begins in the 6th century *(p. 113, MGG)*.

From la rue Saint-Jacques, bus 24 turns left onto le boulevard Saint-Germain, which leads back to the river. There the bus turns right onto le Quai Saint-Bernard. As the bus turns, look right at the new and very modern **Arab World Studies Building** on the cam-

113

pus of l'Université de Paris. Both these institutions are situated on the site of old wine cellars. Wines brought from Bourgogne and the Rhone via canal and the Seine were unloaded and stored here.

After a short run along *le quai,* the bus passes (on the right) **le Jardin des Plantes**, created in 1626 as a royal garden of medicinal herbs. An interesting natural history museum and a menagerie are located here as well. In this area are planted examples of every kind of tree that grows in Paris *(p. 154, MGG).*

When the bus reaches **la Place Valhubert** (where la Gare d'Austerlitz, the train station serving the southwest of France, is found), it turns left and crosses the river on le Pont d'Austerlitz. Back on the Right Bank, it jogs onto le boulevard Diderot, which leads to la Gare de Lyon.

Get off here. You can take either bus 63 to the Trocadéro or bus 87 to la Tour Eiffel.

2. Bus 29: Gare Saint-Lazare to Porte de Montempoivre

Operates weekdays from 6:30 a.m. to 8:30 p.m.; no service Sunday or holidays. Average wait between buses: 6 to 10 minutes weekdays; 9 to 10 minutes Saturday.

La Gare Saint-Lazare, built in 1836, was the first train station in Paris. The passenger platforms, painted by Monet in 1877, have not changed drastically, although the station was modernized in 1930.

From la Gare Saint-Lazare, bus 29 takes la rue Auber to **l'Opéra**. (For a good description of l'Opéra, *see p. 80, MGG.*) The bus then crosses the large open place de l'Opéra and enters la rue du 4-Septembre. This was the day the Fourth Republic was proclaimed in 1870.

On la rue du 4-Septembre, bus 29 passes directly in front of **la Bourse**, the Paris stock exchange, which, like the New York exchange, is housed in a Corinthian peristyle building *(p. 123, MGG).* There the bus turns right on the narrow little street of Notre Dame des Victoires. The street leads to a small strange triangular square with the delightful name **la place des Petit Pères**. The fathers were perhaps so named because they wore no shoes (this is the site of the Monastery of the Barefoot Augustines).

The bus usually moves very fast here, but if you look back you can catch a glimpse of the **church of Notre Dame des Victoires**. Students and businessmen often pray for victory here before an examination or a business deal. **La rue Vide Gousset** (Pick-

114

pocket Street!) leads into the beautiful circular **place des Victoires**. An equestrian statue of Louis XIV, the Sun King, stands in the center *(p. 123, MGG)*.

From la place des Victoires the number 29 turns onto la rue Etienne Marcel and remains on it until it changes its name, first to la rue aux Ours (of the bears) then to **Grenier-Saint-Lazare**. This street lost one side when la rue Etienne-Marcel was lengthened. It is what is left of the old rue Garnier-Saint-Lazare of 1315. The name comes from a family who owned property here and from the Convent of Saint-Ladre (Saint-Lazare). There are some nice old houses on the right.

The bus next turns right onto la rue Beaubourg, which quickly changes its name to la rue du Renard and passes by the back of **le Pompidou** (Paris' premier modern art museum, itself a major contemporary masterpiece or eyesore, depending on your perspective). From this street the bus turns left onto **la rue des Francs Bourgeois**. This interesting name was given to the street in 1334 when several poorhouses were built on it. The people who lived in them were known as *francs biyrgeois* (those Frenchmen who pay no tax).

As the bus crosses la rue des Archives, note the large mansion on the corner—it is called l'Hôtel de Soubise. Next to it is l'Hôtel de Rohan. These buildings are the storage places of **les Archives Nationales Français** *(p. 86-87, MGG)*.

When traveling in the opposite direction—*toward* la Gare Saint-Lazare—the bus takes la rue Saint-Giles, la rue de la Perle (the stop for the Picasso museum), and la rue Michel le Compte (from a 13th-century play on words meaning "paid up"). These are all very old and interesting streets.

Shortly after les Archives, the bus passes (on the left) **l'Hôtel Carnavalet**, a Renaissance mansion (1544) redone by Mansart in 1655. It was the home of the Marquise de Sévigné and today is the museum of the city of Paris *(p. 83, MGG)*.

Number 29 crosses la rue de Turenne and enters **la place des Vosges**. This is an extraordinary square of red brick homes built by Henri IV for himself, his queen, and members of his court. Unfortunately, he did not live to see it completed. He was assassinated in 1610, five years after the work began. From the bus you can see the ground-level arcades circling *la place*, and you will want to spend some time here *(p. 83, MGG)*.

Then the bus emerges onto **le boulevard Beaumarchais**—
the very last of *les grands boulevards*. It turns right and proceeds to the historic **place de la Bastille** *(p. 153, MGG)*.

Keep your eyes open as you go through this part of Paris; it is

115

changing rapidly. While the new Opéra is being built (look for the cranes on one side of the square), many old lofts and low-cost residences are being sold, renovated, and resold. The population changes as the neighborhood attracts young artists. (For historic references, *see p. 153, MGG*.)

Bus 29 takes la rue de Lyon to le boulevard Diderot in front of **la Gare de Lyon**. The 300-foot-high campanile with four clocks was added in 1899 when the original station, built in 1852, was reconstructed. The station has been enlarged several times, and recently a freight station was added to the complex. A hotel has been built against the south side of the passenger station. La Gare de Lyon, the taking-off point for the la Côte d'Azur and Italy, has a beautiful restaurant (le Train Bleu) on the first floor. It's done in the turn-of-the-century style and is named after the famous train that once ran between Calais and Nice.

After la Gare de Lyon, the 29 passes through a workingman's quarter, an area not as a rule visited by tourists. The neighborhood, architecture, and squares are interesting, however. **La Fontaine des Lions** (Lion Fountain) by David in la place Félix Eboue should be noted.

One of the most fascinating (and horrible) souvenirs of the Terror during the French Revolution is the **Picpus cemetery** (at 35 rue Picpus). In the nearby **place de la Nation** no less than 1,308 people, including 16 Carmelite nuns, were guillotined in 1794. Their bodies were tossed into a communal grave, to become known as **Martyrs' Field**. Later, the grave was enclosed by a wall, and a cemetery was opened where relatives of the guillotined could be buried. **Lafayette's grave** is here, and, surprisingly, an American flag remained on it throughout the Nazi Occupation. You'll also see the **chapel of the Carmelites**, who have maintained a continuous prayer 24 hours a day for nearly 200 years.

3. Bus 30: Trocadéro to Gare de L'est

Operates weekdays 7 a.m. to 8:30 p.m.; no service Sunday or holidays. Average wait between buses: 4 to 7 minutes weekdays; 12 to 15 minutes Saturday.

You can reach le Trocadéro by the number 63 from the Left Bank, the numbers 30 and 32 from the Right Bank, and metro lines 9 and 6 from the Left Bank.

Before boarding the bus, take a walk out onto the plaza overlooking la Tour Eiffel, **le Champ de Mars**, and **l'Ecole Militaire**. (It was here Hitler did a jig for the newsreel cameras after the

116

fall of France in 1940.)

The museums in **le Palais de Chaillot**, across the Seine from la Tour Eiffel, are all worth a visit: the Museum of Man, the Maritime Museum, and one with a collection of ancient French monuments. There's also the famous Paris Cinémathèque. The entrance is at the east end on the riverside of *le palais*. (For details and a history of le Trocadéro, *see p. 48, MGG.*)

Bus number 30 takes l'avenue Kleber, a fine old residential street that leads into la place de l'Etoile (Charles de Gaulle). At *la place* is **l'Arc de Triomphe**, built from 1806 to 1836 to celebrate the glory of the Napoleonic armies. The most famous of the sculptures that adorn it is called "The departure of the 1792 volunteers," better known as la Marseillaise. Also notable is the flame of remembrance on the tomb of the unknown soldier of World War I. It is relit each night. A good view of Paris can be had from the top of the arch. (For more details on la place de l'Etoile, *see p. 47, MGG.*)

The bus proceeds down the wide shaded avenue de Wagram. **La place de la Porte des Ternes** is a former Paris tollgate that led to the village of Ternes outside the city wall.

Number 30 bus turns right on le boulevard de Courcelles running along the north side of **le Parc Monceau** *(p. 161, MGG).* Le boulevard de Courcelles loses its name and elegance when it becomes le boulevard des Batignolles. Until 1860, this too was a village outside the Paris wall. Today it cuts through the **le Quartier Europe** of Paris, so named because many streets there bear the names of European cities. The Batignolles ends at **la place Clichy**, which is the southern boundary of Montmartre. The bus takes la rue Caulaincourt into le boulevard de Clichy.

La place Blanche (so called because of the white plaster of paris once mined beneath it) and **la place Pigalle** (named after a sculptor) are famous for their night life, though today it is not as it was during the time of Toulouse-Lautrec. At 100 blvd. de Clichy, le Théâtre de Deux Anes is situated on the site of le Cabaret des Truands (Thieves' Tavern). At number 68, le Caveau du Chat Noir has disappeared, and le Théâtre de Dix Heures is where la Lune Rousse night club once stood. Many post-Impressionist artists lived in and painted this neighborhood. The little winding streets that go up the hillside lead to the picturesque old village of **Montmartre**—a tourist haven but still worth visiting.

At Pigalle, *le boulevard* changes its name to **Rochechouart** (the 18th-century abbess of Montmartre). August Renoir set up his last Paris studio at number 57, and number 84 was the locale of Aristide Bruant's cabaret, made famous by so many Toulouse-

117

Lautrec posters.

The pleasant little green square of **Anvers** is on the site of the Montmartre slaughterhouse. From here (up la rue de Steinkirque) you can get to la place Saint-Pierre and la place Willette—just below the butte that le Sacré-Coeur is built on. There is a new art museum in the steel and glass building that was once le Marché Saint-Pierre (a fabric market). On the left of la place Willette there is a **funicular** that will take you to le Sacré Coeur for one metro ticket or for free if you have a metro pass.

Bus number 30 turns right off le boulevard Rochechouart onto **le boulevard Magenta**. At number 81, le Marché Saint-Quentin operates in an old covered market.

The bus continues down the boulevard, passing **la Gare du Nord** (on the left) and turns into la rue 8-Mai-1945 (the day World War II ended in Europe), which leads to **la Gare de l'Est**. This is the largest railroad station in Paris. It was enlarged and rebuilt from 1895 to 1899 and redone from 1924 to 1931. It serves the east of France and Europe. It was from here that troops in both World Wars left for the front. There is a painting in the entrance by an American, Albert Herter, titled "The depart of French troops on the 1st of August 1914." During the Nazi occupation, deportees for the concentration camps were herded through this station.

At la Gare de l'Est, you can catch bus number 32 for a scenic trip to **la Porte de Passy**.

The garden of artists.

4. Bus 32: Gare de L'Est to Porte de Passy

Operates weekdays from 7 a.m. to 8:30 p.m.; no service Sunday or holidays. Average wait between buses: 3 to 10 minutes weekdays; 10 to 11 minutes Saturday.

This bus line does not take the same route in each direction. To get the most from it, take it both ways. It travels completely across Paris' Right Bank from the northeast to dead west at la Porte de Passy.

In 1883 a contract was

118

drawn up in Constantinpole between the Wagons-Lits (Europe's equivalent to the Pullman Company) and the various railways operating between there and Paris. This agreement created l'Express d'Orient, which became the most famous train in Europe. The many versions of l'Express d'Orient left Paris from **la Gare de l'Est**. The station was one of the most important railroad connections in Europe, and it is architecturally the most interesting of the five Paris rail terminals.

The number 32 bus leaves la Gare de l'Est, crosses le boulevard Magenta, and, after a short distance on le boulevard de Strasbourg, turns into **la rue de Paradis**. This is the street for crystal and glassware, and both wholesale and retail showrooms line both sides. The famous glass maker Baccarat has an interesting museum of glass at number 30*bis*. At number 18 (a fascinating building, once the headquarters of a china and porcelain company) is now located the museum of advertising and posters *(p. 165, MGG)*.

Next the bus passes the **church of the Trinity**, an Italian Renaissance structure built in the mid-19th century. Continuing, the 32 crosses **le Quartier Europe** of Paris, where the streets bear the names of major European cities. Descending la rue d'Amsterdam it passes **la Gare Saint-Lazare** (described in the two previous itineraries). After *la gare* it turns into le boulevard Haussmann, passing (on the left) **la place Louis XVI**, a cemetery during the Revolution and the site of the final resting place of some interesting, if headless, revolutionary characters *("Expiatory Chapel," p. 157, MGG)*.

On the right is the Byzantine and Italianate **church of Saint-Augustin**, built between 1860 and 1868. Cast-iron beams were used for the inner structure. The architect was Baltard, who built the cast-iron and glass pavilions in the old les Halles market. The statue of Joan of Arc in the square is a replica of the one in Reims.

When coming from la Porte de Passy toward la Gare de l'Est, the bus takes les Champs-Elysées and l'avenue Matignon, crossing **la rue du faubourg-St.-Honoré**. This route passes through some of the most expensive real estate in Paris. The neighborhood is noted for fancy shops and art galleries.

The next point of interest as the bus follows the commercial rue la Boetie (pronounced "la bwassie") is the church of Saint-Philippe-du-Roule. The name comes from the village of Roule, once located on the site of la rue du faubourg-Saint Honoré *(p. 91, MGG)*.

The 32 then crosses les Champs-Elysées about midway between l'Etoile (l'Arc de Triomphe) and le Rond-Point *(p. 44, MGG)*.

On the opposite side of the Champs-Elysées, la Boetie first takes the name of Pierre-Charron, then crossing l'avenue George V it becomes **Pierre-1er-de-Serbie**. Pierre Karadjardjevic of Serbia attended the French equivalent of West Point at Saint-Cyr and became a hero in World War I fighting with the French. The street was named for him in 1918.

A few blocks after crossing the wide tree-lined avenue Marceau you will see le Palais Galliera (on the left, 10 rue-Pierre-1er-de-Serbie). This beautiful Italian Renaissance mansion now houses the city's **museum of fashion and costume**.

The bus then enters **la place d'Iéna**. In the center stands an equestrian statue of **George Washington**. This was presented to the city of Paris in 1900 by American women "In memory of the friend-ship and fraternal aid given by France to their fathers during the struggle for independence." The Guimet Museum is also on la place d'Iéna. It contains an interesting collection of oriental art *(p. 136, MGG)*.

From l'avenue d'Iéna the bus goes up l'avenue President Woodrow Wilson (named in 1918) to le Trocadéro, where stands le **Palais de Chaillot**. It was built in 1937 for the Universal Exhibition *(p. 48, MGG)*.

The bus then makes a slight jog from the west side of le Trocadéro onto l'avenue Paul Doumer and enters the neighborhood of Passy. In the 18th century, when this was a village about three miles from Paris, **Benjamin Franklin** lived in a cottage here. He installed the first lightning conductor in France on his house. Franklin's popularity in Paris was enormous. He was welcomed by royalty and cheered by crowds wherever he went. He was admired by leaders of society and government, as well as by philosophers, who compared him to Socrates and Newton. He went everywhere wearing an American Quaker costume with either a fur hat or a little round one, a brown cloth coat, and large spectacles. When news of his death reached Paris in 1790, the government declared three days of national mourning. L'avenue Franklin, which leads to le Palais de Chaillot, is named after him.

At the **Ranelagh gardens**, the first manned balloon ascent was made in 1783. Benjamin Franklin was among those who watched men leave the planet and soar over the Seine for a 25-minute flight that went about five miles downwind.

Before the bus reaches its terminal at la Porte de Passy (Louis Boilly), you will find le **Musée de Marmatton** *(p. 164, MGG)*. It's a fabulous collection of 65 Monet paintings.

From la Porte de Passy, it is not far to la Porte de la Muette, the end of the 63 line. This is a good way to return to midtown or to take your next city bus sightseeing trip.

120

5. Bus 58: Hôtel de Ville to Vanues

Operates weekdays 7 a.m. to 8:30 p.m.; no service Sunday or holidays.
Average wait between buses: 5 to 9 minutes weekdays; 6 to 9 minutes
Saturday.

Bus number 58 leaves its terminal on l'avenue Victoria in front
of **l'Hôtel de Ville** *(p. 87, MGG)* and jogs to la rue de Rivoli. En
route it passes la place St. Jacques and its tower, built at the beginning of the 16th century. The tower is all that is left of the **church
of Saint-Jacques de la Boucherie** *(p. 68, MGG)*.

The bus stays on la rue de Rivoli just to la rue du Pont Neuf, a
narrow street that separates the two buildings of the Samaritaine
department store.

The 58 then crosses **le Pont Neuf** *(p. 68-69, MGG)*. A 17th-
century diarist wrote that the bridge "consists of 12 arches, in the
midst of which ends the point of an island, on which are built hand-
some houses....On the bridge...there is one large passage for coaches,
and two for foot passengers three or four feet higher, and of convenient
breadth for 8 or 10 to go abreast. On the middle of this stately bridge,
on one side stands the famous statue of Henry the Great on horse-
back....The statue and horse are of copper, the work of the great John
de Bologna and sent from Florence by Ferdinand the first, and Cosmo
the second, uncle and cousin of Marie de Medici, the wife of King
Henry."

Behind the statue and at a lower level are the gardens of le Vert-
Galant (a nickname for Henri IV, meaning "lusty old boy"). This is
the lowest point in Paris. Opposite the statue is la place Dauphine,
named in honor of Louis XIII by his father, Henri IV. Little is left of
this triangular *place*, once the setting for a beautiful pair of matched
houses *(p. 62, MGG)*.

Reaching the Left Bank, the bus turns first right, then left entering la rue Guénégaud. On *le quai* at the corner of this narrow street is
l'Hôtel des Monnaies, the French mint. Built in the 18th century,
it has remained in mint condition. The magnificent interior is open to
the public *(p. 137, MGG)*.

The bus then turns left onto **la rue Mazarine**. The old buildings along these streets on the Left Bank survived the era of Napoléon
III and Haussmann, who destroyed many others to make way for traffic
arteries and *boulevards*. Their unrealized plan to extend la rue de
Rennes all the way to le Pont Neuf would have eliminated these
streets.

The bus passes the corner of la rue Saint-André-des-Arts and its
extension, la rue de Buci. **La rue de Buci** was originally a path

121

leading through the fortifications built by Philippe Auguste from the abbey of St. Germain to le Petit Pont.

The name **Saint-André-des-Arts** was originally Saint-André-des-Arcs, referring to the passage through the city wall. The mispronunciation and consequent name change had much to do with the art schools in the neighborhood.

(The 58 returns on **la rue Dauphine**, originally a waterway. It was the moat of the Philippe Auguste wall.)

The bus then takes la rue de l'Ancienne Comédie (from la Comédie Française). At number 13 is **le Café Procope**. The first *café* in Paris, it's now a restaurant.

Crossing le boulevard Saint-Germain at le carrefour de l'Odeon, we take la rue de Condé to **la rue Vaugirard**. This long street (the longest in Paris) was built on the Roman road to Dreux. Immediately on the left is **le Palais de Luxembourg**. This once royal residence surrounded by gardens was built by Marie de Medici in about 1615. Since 1958 it has been the meeting place of the French Senate. **Le Jardin de Luxembourg** is one of the most beautiful in Paris. An orangerie protects several score of palm trees and tropical shrubs during the winter months. They are all moved into the garden during the summer *(p. 119-120, MGG)*.

The number 58 leaves the Vaugirard to take la rue Guynemer that runs along the west edge of le Jardin de Luxembourg. It turns off onto la rue Vavin and crosses le boulevard Raspail to le boulevard Montparnasse, where it turns right. At this point the bus is directly in front of the famous Café Coupole. This renowned establishment opened in the 1920s when Montparnasse was very fashionable and the meeting place of many avant-garde artists. There were four popular *cafés* at that time: **la Coupole**, today a restaurant/*brasserie*; directly across the street **le Café Select**, still *un café* much as it was 60 years ago; next to le Select, on the corner of le boulevard Raspail, **la Rotonde**, now a movie house and tea room; and across le boulevard Montparnasse from the site of la Rotonde, **le Dôme,** which has become a fashionable (and very good) fish restaurant. These four *cafés* of the 1920s were the rendez-vous of cosmopolitan bohemians, especially among Russian refugees and Americans fleeing New York and the Midwest. Almost any day one could meet Modigliani, Picasso, Matisse, Chagall, or Cendrars here.

A bit farther along on le boulevard Montparnasse the bus enters **la place du 19-juin-1940**. The date commemorates deGaulle's famous broadcast from London imploring the people of France to continue to fight. Today the huge business complex of **Maine-Montparnasse** looms over the square. It stands where the modest Montparnasse train station once was. The tower, 57 floors high, affords one of the best views of Paris. (In part because the ugly tower itself cannot be seen from here!)

The bus takes la rue du Départ (at one time along the east side of the Montparnasse train station) to **l'avenue du Maine** amid towering buildings. These were built during Pompidou's term of office when "modernization" meant "Manhattanization." From here, the bus turns right onto **la rue des Plantes**, a pleasant old street in an area where old streets are a threatened few. At number 66, an order of nuns founded in the 13th century operates the **l'hôpital Notre Dame de Bon Secours** (our lady of perpetual help).

On la rue des Plantes, the 58 reaches le boulevard Brune, an outer *boulevard*. One block south of the la Porte Didot bus stop you will find a small, delightful flea market on Saturday and Sunday. This is one of the last markets in Paris where "old junk" is sold.

The bus then leaves Paris for the **suburb of Vanves**, home of le Lycée Michelet. This *lycée* (high school) is situated in the 17th-century château of the royal Condé family and surrounded by a vast park.

From le boulevard Brune you can get *la Petite Ceinture* to another porte or a return bus number 59. Going west on *la P.C.*, you reach la Porte de Versailles; east is la Porte d'Orléans.

6. Bus 63: Gare de Lyon to Porte de La Muette

Operates daily from 7 a.m. to midnight. Average wait between buses: 4 to 6 minutes Monday to Friday; 8 to 10 minutes Saturday; 8 to 15 minutes Sunday.

The number 63 bus begins its trip on la rue de Bercy in front of the lower level exit from la Gare de Lyon.

La Gare de Lyon is the station built by the famous PLM (Paris-Lyon-Méditerranée) railroad when it was privately owned. It is the most elaborate of the five Paris stations, with a 200-foot-high campanile with four clocks. A restaurant on the second floor overlooking the departure platforms is called le Train Bleu after the now-extinct Calais-Nice overnight luxury train.

After leaving the station, the number 63 turns onto le boulevard Diderot and crosses the Seine on le Pont d'Austerlitz. It follows le Quai Saint-Bernard, passing first **le Jardin des Plantes** (on the left) with a glimpse of the animals in the menagerie, then **l'Université de Paris** (la Faculté des Sciences is a cluster of unattractive high-rises), and finally, as the bus turns onto **la rue des Fosses**

Saint-Bernard, the new and equally unattractive glass and steel **Arab World Studies Building.** (La rue des Fosses Saint-Bernard refers to the moat along the wall built by Philippe Augustus near la Porte Saint-Bernard. The street was built on the filled-in moat in 1670.)

At the end of la rue des Fosses Saint-Bernard, the 63 swings west onto **la rue des Ecoles.** This is called the street of schools because schools and colleges have been located along it since the Middle Ages. The oldest is probably le College des Bon-Enfants, which dates back to 1254. The street itself was named in 1857. The Sorbonne, founded in 1258, and le Collège de France, founded in 1530 by François 1er, are situated at the other end of the street *(p. 108-109, MGG).* On the right after la rue St. Jacques is the magnificent **Hôtel de Cluny,** an example of medieval French domestic architecture. It houses le Musée de Cluny, which is devoted to the arts and crafts of the Middle Ages *(p. 115-116, MGG).*

After crossing le boulevard Saint-Michel, the bus jogs through what seems to be an incredibly narrow street for such a big vehicle. This is **la rue de l'Ecole-de-Médecine,** a fabulous street full of history. It was once a Gallo-Roman footpath between two vineyards. Sarah Bernhardt was born at number 5, and at number 20 (in a house since torn down) Marat was stabbed by Charlotte Corday. The convent of les Cordeliers (so-called because they tied their robes closed with heavy cords) was at numbers 15 to 21. In the era of the Revolution, the intellectual revolutionaries' Club des Cordeliers had its headquarters in the same building *(p. 117, MGG).*

When the 63 emerges from la rue de l'Ecole-de-Médecine it is in the place popularly known as **Odéon.** However, since 1968, it has officially been called **la place Henri-Mondor.** From here the bus jogs left, then right onto **la rue Saint-Sulpice,** a pleasant street with many nice shops and hotels. It leads to **la place Saint-Sulpice** in front of the church of the same name *(p. 120, MGG).*

(Traveling in the opposite direction, the number 63 bus remains on le boulevard Saint-Germain for its entire two-mile length (from le Palais Bourbon to le Quai Saint-Bernard). This is one of the wide tree-lined boulevards Haussmann cut through many of the small twisting streets of Paris. In addition to the elegant town houses, it passes through the famous book publishing neighborhood of Saint-Germain-des-Prés. This includes not only the beautiful church, but also the famous literary *cafés* de Flore and des Deux Magots, as well as *la brasserie* Lipp, the denizen of politicians. A bit farther along it passes the garden behind le Musée de Cluny at le boulevard Saint-Michel.)

The west-bound bus continues along the north side of la place

Saint-Sulpice. It turns into **la rue du Vieux-Columbier,** a street named after a dovecote that was described as old in the 13th century. Like almost everything in *le quartier* in the 13th century, the dovecote belonged to the Abbey Saint-Germain (only bishops and higher ranks were allowed to keep pigeons).

Le Vieux-Columbier ends at **la Croix Rouge** (see itinerary of bus 87 for details), where the bus turns left, then right onto le boulevard Raspail. This is a main artery on the Left Bank that was opened piecemeal during the 19th century. At this corner, on the left, is the splendid rococo **Hôtel Lutetia.**

The 63 leaves le boulevard Raspail when it reaches le boulevard Saint-Germain and takes an alley reserved for buses and taxis. This passes through an elegant part of Paris with many **ministries** and **embassies** in beautiful old town houses with walled gardens.

Upon reaching the Seine (and the end of le boulevard Saint-Germain), the 63 is in front of **le Palais Bourbon,** today the meeting place of the national assembly *(p. 132, MGG).* To the right is an excellent view across le Pont Concorde, la place de la Concorde, and the facade of la Madeleine. The bus takes the Left Bank **Quai d'Orsay.** It passes the extension to le Palais Bourbon known as **l'Hôtel Lassay.** This magnificent palace houses the president of the assembly.

When the bus reaches **les Invalides** you have one of the most extensive views in Paris. To your left is the immense green esplanade providing a perfect view of the classically balanced buildings of les Invalides with the dome of the **church of Saint-Louis** behind them *(p. 71, MGG).* To the right is the most beautiful bridge in Paris, **le Pont Alexandre III,** and on the other side of the river are **le Petit Palais** and **le Grand Palais** *(p. 45, MGG).*

After such splendid views, even the tree-lined *quai* with its beautiful town houses seems a little dull. At number 63-65 stands a red stone church that looks like thousands in towns or cities across America. It is the **American Church of Paris** (not to be confused with the American Cathedral on l'avenue George V). The church is on the corner of la rue Jean-Nicot—the street named for the French diplomat who introduced tobacco to France and gave his name to nicotine.

The 63 then crosses to the Right Bank on le Pont de l'Alma *(p. 135, MGG).* This bridge, rebuilt a few years ago, originally had four statues of French *légionnaires.* One, a Zouave, became popular with Parisians who used him as a water-level gauge (feet covered, high water; knees wet, slight flooding conditions; butt of rifle, serious flood).

On the Right Bank, the bus enters the large, busy place de l'Alma, where seven streets merge at the river's edge. Those on the right lead to the fashionable part of les Champs-Elysées neighborhood, those on the left to the expensive 16th *arrondissement* residential area.

From there the bus turns onto l'avenue President Wilson, passing the modern art collection of the city of Paris (housed in **le Palais de Tokyo**) on the left. On the right one can see, past a grilled iron fence and across a beautiful garden, **le Palais Galleria,** the city's museum of costume and fashion.

Halfway up the hill, in the center of la place d'Iéna is a statue of **George Washington.** It was given in 1900 to the French people by "the women of the United States."

Le Trocadéro and **le Palais de Chaillot** are the next stops, and it's worth getting down for a look at the three museums, the view of Paris, and, if they are playing, the fountains below the terrace between the buildings *(p. 48, MGG).* It was on this terrace that Hitler was filmed dancing a jig after the fall of France in 1940.

The final stretch of the 63's run is through a rich, not too attractive, and very expensive residential district. There are some old town houses and apartments, as well as some hideous modern structures along les avenues Georges Mandel and Henri Martin. The one interesting point is **la Fontaine Artésienne** in a small square where l'avenue de Victor-Hugo meets l'avenue Henri Martin. Many people of the neighborhood come here daily to fill bottles with this refreshing spring water. Once a common sight in all parts of town, this is the last of its kind in Paris.

The run ends at **la Porte de la Muette.** The name is derived from the word *meute* (which describes a pack of staghounds), as this was the site of a rendezvous lodge for hunters built during the reign of Charles IX (1560-1574).

Jean and his wooden horse.

Nearby in le Jardin du Ranelagh is **le Musée Marmottan,** where there is an exceptional collection of 65 Monet paintings. You can get a number 32 bus in front of the museum.

There is a nearby stop of *la Petite Ceinture*, if you want to get to another *porte* to pick up another bus line. Otherwise you can return to le Trocadéro on the 63, where several other bus lines stop.

7. Bus 75: Pont-Neuf to Porte de Pantin

Operates weekdays from 6:45 a.m. to 8:30 p.m.; no service Sunday or holidays. Average wait between buses: 8 to 10 minutes weekdays; 10 to 15 minutes Saturday.

Bus number 75 takes you on a tour of the northeastern part of Paris, a part that few tourists visit but that is nonetheless interesting. Out in the extremities of the area is a neighborhood known as **la Villette.** It is rapidly becoming a major tourist attraction. The 75 bus will take you to la Porte de Pantin, quite near la Porte de la Villette and within a few hundred feet of the entrance to the new complex there (see below).

The starting point for the number 75's itinerary is on the Right Bank near **le Pont Neuf.** Begun by Henri III in 1578 and finished in 1604 by Henri IV, it is the oldest bridge in Paris. The stone used to build this durable bridge was quarried in Paris and what were then its suburbs *(p. 69, MGG).* At one time a huge water-pumping station existed at the Right Bank foot of the bridge. There was a bas-relief depicting Jesus and the woman of Samaria, who was seen pouring water out of a bucket. It was probably this water pump and its art work that gave the name "Samaritaine" to the neighborhood and particularly to the department store on the site.

Number 75 takes le Quai de la Mégisserie past **le Théâtre du Châtelet** and **le Pont au Change.** The bridge derives its name from the fact that the houses on this street were occupied by goldsmiths and money lenders *(p. 68, MGG).* The bus continues along the same *quai* to **l'Hôtel de Ville** (city hall). The square in front of this magnificently reconstructed building (it was burned during the Commune in 1871) was called **la place Grève.** The unemployed gathered here to demonstrate; thus a strike is called *une grève.* This place was also the site of many executions during the Terror *(p. 67, MGG).*

Next, the bus turns left off *le quai* to pass directly behind l'Hôtel de Ville and then up **la rue des Archives** *(p. 103, MGG).* On the corner of la rue des Quatre-Fils is l'Hôtel de Guénégaud. It houses a museum of hunting (le Musée de la Chasse).

(On the return trip the 75 passes through la rue Beaubourg directly behind le Centre Georges Pompidou.)

At la place du Temple (on the left) and le marché du Temple (on the right), the bus turns left around the square. This is **le Quartier du Temple,** and it has a fascinating history *(p. 171-172, MGG).* The

127

covered market called **le marché du Temple** was built in 1809 on the site after the remains of the old Finnish temple were pulled down. The market is called le Carreau du Temple, and today clothes (*friperies*) are sold here.

The bus then crosses **la place de la République** *(p. 168, MGG)*, built on the site of la Porte du Temple and enlarged in 1880. **Le Canal Saint-Martin,** which tunnels under Paris from the Bastille, emerges here. The 75 bus turns left, and we suddenly find ourselves on *le quai* of a tree-lined canal with high-arched bridges, locks, and towpaths *(p. 169, MGG)*.

The bus turns right as it is routed around **l'Hôpital Saint-Louis.** This hospital was created by Henri IV for victims of the plague, who were overcrowding the only hospital in Paris at that time, **l'Hôtel-Dieu.** Today l'Hôpital Saint-Louis specializes in skin diseases. The Louis XIII-style red-brick buildings date back to the 18th century.

Bus number 75 then turns onto a street with the strange name of **la rue de la Grange-aux-Belles.** The origin of the name is not clear. It is thought it might be from *pelle* or *pellee,* referring to a shed where spades (*pelles*) might have been stored during construction or when a moat was dug nearby. In any case, we do know that at number 53 stood the 13th-century **Gibet de Montfaucon,** the most famous of the king's gallows. Its 16-yard arms served two purposes: to hang those condemned and to exhibit corpses (often beheaded) as examples. In 1954, while excavating for a garage at number 53, two beams believed to be from the gallows were found six feet below the surface.

A bit farther along, **la place du Colonel Fabien** was once known as la place du Combat. Spanish-style bullfights were held here until 1848. The modern building to the right of the bus houses the French Communist Party headquarters.

Shortly past the square, the bus passes along the rim of a large green and hilly reserve. This is **le Parc des Buttes Chaumont,** an interesting public park. The name comes from a 1216 writ that referred to it "*in territario dicto calvo monte,*" which meant "*mont chauve,*" or bare hills. For many years windmills stood on the heights, and stone was quarried for Paris buildings. (The quarries were for gypsum.) Later, it became a city dump until Napoléon III and Haussmann converted it into a delightful park. It has a nice restaurant with a large terrace that makes it a splendid place for a summer lunch.

La mairie, or town hall, of the 19th *arrondissement* can be seen to the left of the bus. An amusing structure, it was built in 1876 in the Flemish style.

The 75 then runs beside the elevated boulevard Périphérique, the

ring road around Paris. Its last stop, l'avenue Jean Jaures, is a short
distance from the entrance to le Parc de la Villette, a museum/park
complex.

La Villette, a suburban village annexed by Paris in 1860, was
for many years famous for its stockyards and *abattoir* (slaughterhouse).
The very expensive *abattoir* built at the end of the 1960s, badly
conceived and practically unusable, was the cause of a government
scandal. Shortly afterward, and before the slaughterhouse was ever in
use, the butchers were moved to the new wholesale food market in
Rungis, leaving 136 acres of real estate, a half-dozen 19th-century iron
and glass pavilions, the useless *abattoir,* and a scattering of small
Victorian buildings. A basin, fed by the Saint-Martin and the Ourcq
canals, borders one side and cuts across the center of the complex.

The entire site is being renovated and reconstructed. The renovated
slaughterhouse has already opened as a "City of Science." Nearby is
the Géode, a sphere of polished steel that houses a 180-degree film
projector. By the end of this year, a public park is scheduled to open.
One-sixth the size of New York City's Central Park, the park will be
equipped with bandstands, restaurants and lunch rooms, playgrounds
and athletic facilities, a greenhouse, an electronic game center, walking malls, gardens, fountains, and open spaces.

Also planned is a "City of Music." La Villette is easily accessible
by two metro stations, one from la Porte de la Villette, the other from
la Porte Pantin. The latter gets you to the center of Paris in less than
20 minutes.

8. Bus 82 Gare du Luxembourg to Neuilly

Operates Monday through Saturday from 7 a.m. to 8:30 p.m.; Sunday
8:30 a.m. to 8:30 p.m. Average wait between buses: 6 to 8 minutes
weekdays; 8 to 10 minutes Saturday; 11 to 19 minutes Sunday.

The number 82 bus travels from le Quartier Latin on the Left
Bank to the American Hospital in Neuilly. It is a long ride (a bit more
than an hour in heavy traffic) but an interesting one.

The bus starts in front of the entrance to le Jardin de Luxembourg
(p. 120, MGG) on the corner of la rue de Medicis and le boulevard
Saint-Michel. Across *le boulevard* you can see the Pantheon at the top
of la rue Soufflot.

At any time of the year **le Jardin de Luxembourg** is worth a
visit. In the spring the flower displays just inside the gates on la rue
de Medicis are sensational. On the other side of the garden (bordering
on la rue Auguste-Comte) there is an extensive orchard of espaliered
fruit trees of many varieties. In the autumn the flower beds around the

basin are in beautiful and colorful bloom.

After passing the gardens, the bus goes up la rue Vavin to le boulevard du Montparnasse (see itinerary of bus number 58 for a description of **Montparnasse** in the 1920s), turns right to reach **la place du 18-Juin-1940.** The date commemorates deGaulle's famous plea from London imploring the French people to continue to fight. The high-rises dominating the square have replaced a modest train station, la Gare Montparnasse. The station has been modernized in the style of New York City's Penn Station and moved back away from its original location. The 57-floor **Tour Montparnasse** affords an excellent view of Paris.

In a straight line, the bus continues to la place Vauban in front of **le Dôme des Invalides,** which tops the church of Saint-Louis, at the rear of l'Hôtel des Invalides. Under le Dôme des Invalides, inside the church, the Emperor Napoléon is buried (*p. 73, MGG*).

The next important square is **la place de l'Ecole Militaire,** built by Louis XV for 500 impoverished gentlemen dedicated to serving in the king's army (*p. 53, MGG*). The **military academy,** with its beautiful 18th-century buildings, is on the left, and the long alley of **le Champ-de-Mars** (the parade ground for l'Ecole Militaire) is on the right. La Tour Eiffel is at the far end of le Champ-de-Mars. Le Palais de Chaillot on le Trocadéro across the Seine is visible under the arch of the tower.

The bus then turns down l'avenue de Suffren and goes along the west side of le Champ-de-Mars to the Seine and **la Tour Eiffel** (*p. 5, MGG*). Directly in front of the tower we cross the river on le Pont de Iéna. In front of the bus play the fountains of le Trocadéro. **Le Palais de Chaillot,** built for the 1937 Universal Exhibition, is an impressive sight. *Le palais* houses several interesting museums.

Next, the bus turns and heads up the hill to la place de Iéna. In the center of the square is an equestrian statue of **George Washington** given to Paris by "the women of the United States" in 1900 as thanks for French help during the American Revolution. On the same square is **le Musée Guimet,** specializing in Asian Art.

The 82 continues to climb up la rue Boissière. At number 4, la rue Hamelin begins. It was on this street that **Marcel Proust** lived and died.

After a short run on l'avenue Kléber, the 82 turns left onto la rue Copernic. This street heads to the circular **place Victor-Hugo** with its fountain, *cafés*, and fine shops. From there the bus takes **l'avenue Raymond Poincaré,** named for the famous mathematician, crossing the beautiful **avenue Foch**—one of the broadest, most expensive avenues of Paris (*p. 159, MGG*).

As the bus enters **la Porte Maillot,** look straight ahead for a good view of **la Défense.** La Défense, not a part of Paris, is so named because it was an important position in the 1871 defense of Paris against the Prussians *(p. 149, MGG).*

The **International Convention Center,** known as the CNIT Building, and **le Palais des Congrès,** a complex of meeting halls, exhibition space, a shopping center, hotels, and a theater, are found at la Porte Maillot.

The 82 bus then enters **Neuilly-sur-Seine.** This suburb, once a quiet residential area with many hospitals and convalescent homes, has grown into a commercial town of service industries. From the bus one sees only the residential district. The entrance to the American Hospital is at the bus terminal.

9. Bus 87: Champ-de-Mars to Porte de Neuilly

Operates weekdays from 7 a.m. to 8:30 p.m.; no service Sunday or holidays. Average wait between buses: 8 to 13 minutes weekdays; 10 to 12 minutes Saturday.

Le Champ-de-Mars, once a military parade ground, is a beautiful stretch of greenery more than a half-mile long that stretches from the Seine to l'Ecole Militaire. For centuries, the space has been used for expositions. La Tour Eiffel at one end of the field was built for the International Exposition of 1889 *(p. 51, MGG).*

The number 87 bus starts near l'avenue de Suffren and passes la Tour Eiffel on its way to **l'avenue de la Bourdonnais.** There it turns right and proceeds to **la place de l'Ecole Militaire.** You can get a close view of the military academy from the right of the bus.

The bus continues on l'avenue Duquesne until it passes behind the **church of Saint François Xavier,** a decorative, 19th-century imitation Romanesque structure. As the bus turns right onto le boulevard des Invalides, look for a view of **le Dôme des Invalides,** the tomb of Napoléon.

(On its return journey, the bus turns north (left) on la rue de Sèvres, then takes la rue de Babylone, where it passes the Pagode movie house, a structure erected by the Chinese Embassy for the 1900 Universal Exhibition.)

La rue de Sèvres is a busy street with many shops, *cafés,* and restaurants. The oldest building is the 17th-century **l'Hôpital Laennec,** formerly a home for incurable women, on the left of the bus. On the wall of the hospital, opposite 97 rue de Sèvres, is an amusing fountain with an Egyptian theme, one of 15 built in various parts of Paris in 1806.

A bit farther along la rue de Sèvres, the bus passes the two large buildings of **le Bon Marché**, one of the largest department stores of Paris and the first department store in the world. After crossing le boulevard Raspail, the 87 passes **le Carrefour de la Croix Rouge**. One would logically associate this with the international Red Cross organization, but no. The name originates from the fact that a massive cesspool and a neighboring hospital for contagious diseases once existed here. Both prompted the monks of the nearby **l'Abbaye Saint-Germain** to put up a warning to passers-by—a red cross.

The bus then takes la rue du Four. As it crosses la rue de Rennes, look left for a view of **Saint-Germain-des-Prés**, one of the oldest and most beautiful churches in Paris.

The name **la rue du Four** comes from the church's 13th-century name, Vicus Furni. The baker of l'Abbaye Saint-Germain was on this street, and people in the neighborhood, risking a fine if found going elsewhere, took their dough to be baked in the abbey oven. The Latin *furni* means "oven," as does the French *four*. La rue de Four ends as it reaches le boulevard Saint-Germain.

The bus stays on *le boulevard*, first passing the Odéon corner then le boulevard Saint-Michel and le Musée Cluny. From the bus you can see the gardens of **le Musée Cluny** and the ruins of Gallo-Roman baths dating back to the second and third centuries. Le Musée Cluny itself is one of the most beautiful mansions and most wonderful museums in Paris *(p. 115-116, MGG)*.

(When the bus returns toward le Champ-de-Mars, it takes la rue des Ecoles and la rue de l'Ecole de Médecine between le boulevard Saint-Michel and l'Odéon. This street was built along a former Gallo-Roman path between two vineyards. The house where Marat was murdered by Charlotte Corday was on this street. From Odéon the 87 takes la rue Saint-Sulpice to la place Saint-Sulpice with its fountain of four bishops who almost ("almost" in French is noteworthy) became cardinals. Thus the name of the fountain: *les quatre points cardinaux* or "the four cardinal points.")

Le boulevard Saint-Germain ends as it reaches the Seine. At this point on your right you will see the sleek new glass-and-metal building of the **Institute of Arab Studies** built on the campus of l'Université de Paris. These buildings are on the site of **old wine halls**, a cluster of thick-walled storehouses where wine coming from all over France into Paris was stored before it was distributed. The wine market itself was built on the site of the teaching abbey of Saint-Victor, which was here from the 11th century until the revolution.

The 87 crosses the Seine on le Pont de Sully. This bridge connects the up-river tip of l'Ile Saint-Louis to both banks. The elegant

17th-and 18th-century town houses can be seen from the bus as it crosses the bridge.

On the Right Bank, the bus is on le boulevard Henri IV, opened in 1866 and cut through the former gardens of the convent of the Célestins. On the right is the barracks housing the mounted **Garde Républicaine.**

The bus then enters **la place de la Bastille.** This was built on the spot where the fortress/prison stood until July 14, 1789. A line of colored paving blocks outline the original site and are visible where le boulevard Henri IV reaches the square *(p. 153-154, MGG).*

On the southeast corner of the square, a half-dozen high cranes are at work in a space cleared of buildings. The new **Opéra** is being built, and plans are being made to inaugurate the building on Bastille Day, July 14, 1989.

From the Bastille, number 87 takes la rue de Lyon to the train station, **la Gare de Lyon.** From here it goes into the part of Paris just east of la Gare de Lyon known as **Bercy.** Once Bercy was a charming village, a thriving river port, and a wine market. It was famous for its *guinguettes*—road houses with gardens for drinking and dancing. Since the beginning of this century, Bercy has been a workingman's quarter consisting mostly of rail freight yards. But along the quays a mammoth sports arena was recently built, and a new building for the ministry of finance is being completed. A small part of the old wine halls still exist; cobblestoned tree-lined streets, thick-walled stock houses, and great casks and barrels everywhere recall greater days.

The bus takes **l'avenue General Michel Bizot** and **la rue de Wattignies** as it doubles back. Both of these streets were created as Bercy grew during the 19th century.

Mr. Bus Stop

Jean-Claude Decaux, a self-made man, owns 80% of an enterprise that does an annual business of 860-million francs. He offers cities *l'autobus* shelters, large clear neighborhood maps placed conveniently near metro exits and bus stops, animated signs that give municipal news, weather reports, and the correct time, public toilets that are mechanically scoured after each use, and large easy-to-see directional signs routing traffic around town. In exchange for the bus stops, which he erects free of charge, Decaux gets exclusive use of valuable advertising space and contracts for the other items. He now has installations in 660 cities around the world, including Moscow where there is no advertising. His ambition is to sell his idea in the United States,

but, he says, protectionism, licensing, and a general lack of coopera-
tion are "ruthless" obstacles. Not to mention the competition!

Getting Out of Paris on the SNCF

The trains of France are a great pleasure—they leave and arrive on
time. First-class seats are a bit larger and softer and are spaced farther
apart than those in second-class. In addition, the first-class compartments have only six places instead of eight. But one can travel with
great comfort in second-class. If traveling by *couchette* (a sleeping car
with tiered bunks), there are only four bunks in first-class and six in
second-class. Prices vary enormously, depending on your choice of
travel. Two people on le Train Bleu (which leaves Paris at 9:46 p.m.
and arrives in Nice at 7:56 a.m.) can pay $365 for first-class or just
$90 for second-class *couchettes*. People under 26 or over 60 are
entitled to half fares with the purchase of either *une carte jeune* or *une
carte vermeille*. These can be purchased at any railroad station upon
presentation of a passport. The half fares are offered on weekdays
(marked in blue on the calendar given with the card) and are for either
first- or second-class travel.

Paris' five train stations are well-organized. Each has *une salle
d'accueil* where you are given a number upon arrival and told at which
group of *guichets* (windows) you will be served. Then you sit and
wait with your eye on the lighted numbers by those windows. Unless
it is just before a holiday period, the wait is never long. One tip:
There seem to be fewer people at la Gare d'Austerlitz than at the other
stations. Once at your *guichet* you can get your card, ticket, and
reservation. Visa credit cards are accepted. When taking a train, the
ticket (not the reservation) must be perforated before boarding. This is
done by sticking either end of the ticket into an orange-colored
machine (*un composteur*). *Les composteurs* are found in all the
stations just at the entrance to train platforms.

Hiking in France

The French hiking trails (*les grandes randonnées*) are marked and
cover every part of the country. Hiking provides an ideal French vaca-
tion at a very low cost. Maps are available, and an excellent guide
called *Gîtes et Refuges en France* by Annick and Serge Mouraret (Editions Créer, rue Jean Amariton, 63340 Nonette, FF65) lists overnight
stops and eating places. The guide leads hikers to *gîtes,* or dormi-
tories, costing from FF20 to FF40 a night; meals are from FF30 to
FF50. The guide is available at a bookshop called Astrolabe (46 rue de
Provence, 9th).